WHAT PEOPLE ARE SAYING ABOUT

"Let *Guarded* inspire you to live a life of deep conviction and purposeful intention. This book is a source of encouragement, showing that a well-guarded heart is not only life-giving but also a fountain of blessings to others. Readers are invited to reconsider what it means to be guarded. It's not just about defense; it's about making intentional choices that align with God's wisdom and purpose for your life. Through captivating stories, reflections, and practical advice, you'll learn the art of setting boundaries, making decisions with discernment, and creating a space where God's best can flourish."

—*Pastor Kimberly Petree*
Citygate Church

"Above all else guard your heart."

"It is that simple yet so complex. Throughout this 'must read' book, *Guarded*, Melissa breaks down just how intricate our hearts are and provides applicable steps to ensure what flows from it is beautiful! Each chapter is packed full of truth, real life stories from trusted friends, and her heart passionately believing that you too can live guarded. With a world committed to keeping us distracted she brings each reader back to the center-foundational truth to live a life of freedom. *Guarded* is for anyone, in any season. If your heart is beating–pick up *Guarded* and never be the same!"

—*Jessica Noe*
Executive Director of Operations
The Avenue Church

"Melissa Graham's heart spills out in language form onto the pages of *Guarded*. With grace and wisdom intertwined, she provides life-giving information about how our entire existence—spiritual, emotional, and physical—is tied to the health of our hearts. The psalmist wrote in Proverbs 4:23 that the heart is the source of life, and this book proves that to be true. Let down your guard and allow the pages of this book to land on your heart, and you will be forever transformed."

—*Pastor Stephanie Harrison*
The Kingdom Center Church and Founder of Unbecoming Me

"Truly impactful books are not just written; they are first lived, then written. Each lesson on the page must first be carved like a steppingstone on the path of a life lived in the trenches, the battlefields, the fog, and the valleys – as well as mountain tops, victory dances, and banquets. Author, Melissa Graham has earned the right to instruct you in guarding your soul. In *Guarded* she delves into a profound life question: How are you protecting your heart to live with purpose? Life is rife with dream stealers and toxic relationships, but Melissa provides guidance on overcoming these challenges and embracing the life God intended—one free of emotional toxins. For those seeking clarity and direction, this book is essential. Begin your journey today with *Guarded* and steer towards a life of freedom and purpose."

—*Bryan Cutshall, Th.D.*
President, ISOW Bible College

"I found *Guarded* to be a book which is relevant to my own life in so many ways. It is a must-read for everyone, regardless of age or walk of life. I believe that you will find yourself reflected within the book's pages, guided by the Spirit of God, and Word of God through Melissa Graham's insights. It highlights the importance of recognizing the value of entrusting one's heart to a higher power, Jesus Christ.

Furthermore, while this book emphasizes the thought that the choice to guard one's heart ultimately lies within the individual, *Guarded* serves as a resource that highlights the power of the Spirit of God and God's Word in preserving hearts through life's various challenges and seasons. Overall, I believe that this book serves as a guide to understanding the significance of where one places their trust and the role of faith in safeguarding the heart."

—*Ron K. Martin*
Church of God Administrative Bishop

"Most people believe you should be careful of who and what is allowed in your life but lack the necessary tools to guard the heart, the place integral to your success and survival. In her book, *Guarded,* Melissa Graham takes you on a journey to help you protect the very thing that determines the course of your whole life. This book challenges you to take an honest inventory of your heart as it currently stands and equips you with the knowledge to protect it from anything that could ruin your future!"

—*Justin Graham,*
Pastor, The Avenue Church

MELISSA GRAHAM
GUARDED

guarded

Copyright © 2024 by Melissa Graham

Published by AVAIL

All rights reserved. No portion of this book may be reproduced, stored in a retrieval system, or transmitted in any form or by any means—electronic, mechanical, photocopy, recording, scanning, or other—except for brief quotations in critical reviews or articles, without prior written permission of the author.

Unless otherwise specified all Scripture quotations are taken from the Holy Bible, New International Version®. Copyright © 1973, 1978, 1984, 2011 by Biblica, Inc.™ Used by permission of Zondervan. All rights reserved worldwide. www.zondervan.com. The "NIV" and "New International Version" are trademarks registered in the United States Patent and Trademark Office by Biblica, Inc.™ | Scripture quotations marked CEV are taken from the Contemporary English Version Bible (CEV), Copyright © 1995 by American Bible Society | Scripture quotations marked ESV are from The ESV® Bible (The Holy Bible, English Standard Version®), copyright © 2001 by Crossway, a publishing ministry of Good News Publishers. Used by permission. All rights reserved. | Scripture quotations marked HCSB are taken from the Holman Christian Standard Bible®, Used by Permission HCSB ©1999, 2000, 2002, 2003, 2009 Holman Bible Publishers. Holman Christian Standard Bible®, Holman CSB®, and HCSB® are federally registered trademarks of Holman Bible Publishers. | Scripture quotations marked KJV are taken from the King James Version of the Bible. Public domain. | Scripture quotations marked NKJV are taken from the New King James Version®. Copyright © 1982 by Thomas Nelson. Used by permission. All rights reserved. | Scripture quotations marked NLT are taken from the Holy Bible, New Living Translation, copyright © 1996, 2004, 2015 by Tyndale House Foundation. Used by permission of Tyndale House Publishers, Inc., Carol Stream, Illinois 60188. All rights reserved. |

For foreign and subsidiary rights, contact the author.

Cover design by: Sara Young
Bio photo by: Tonya Damron
Cover photo by: Meshelle Robbins (The Avenue Church Photography Team)

ISBN: 978-1-964794-18-1   1 2 3 4 5 6 7 8 9 10

Printed in the United States of America

MELISSA GRAHAM
GUARDED

Building a Life of Purpose
by Stewarding Your Heart Well

DEDICATION

To my best friend and husband, Justin—your friendship and love remind me daily to intentionally protect what God has given us. Thank you for standing beside me; you have cheered me on to be who God has called me to be. You guide and guard my heart well! I love you with my whole heart!

To my daughter, Jocelyn—you are the definition of joy. Me and you always and forever. Your heart is a beautiful gift to the world! I am cheering you on as you step out into your calling this season. Thank you for believing in me in this new venture! I can't wait to read all the books you author. I Love You More Than Anything You Say.

To my son, Judah—you define passion. Life with you is so much fun. I am your biggest fan! Your heart is marked with promise. You have a definite purpose in the Kingdom. I am excited to watch you run with excellence. Your strength and discipline inspire me. Thank you for cheering me on. I Love You More Than Anything You Say.

To my parents, Ron and Roshelle Martin—your stewardship over my heart sets me up to succeed. Thank you for being the rare parents who are fully invested in your children. I love you.

Contents

Acknowledgments xi

Foreword xiii

Introduction 15

CHAPTER 1. Heart Central 17

CHAPTER 2. My Heart, My Responsibility 35

CHAPTER 3. Echo 61

CHAPTER 4. Heart Invaders 85

CHAPTER 5. Heart On Fire 123

CHAPTER 6. Guarded to Gain 145

CHAPTER 7. Heart Rhythm 177

CHAPTER 8. Shame-Free Zone 201

CHAPTER 9. Matters of the Heart 213

CHAPTER 10. Leaders Who Fall 237

Guarded Review: Pulse Report 253

ACKNOWLEDGMENTS

Thank you to my incredible Avenue staff and church family! I hope my actions have shown you how much I love and appreciate you. But let me remind you with words: You all are the best team EVER! I love you! Thank you for being a part of my story; you make my heart better.

Jessica Noe, you have invested countless hours into the Guarded brand. Thank you for making sure the vision God put in our hearts looks, sounds, and feels excellent. Your heart for God and the team is ALL IN no matter the season of ministry. Thank you for being the first to offer to read the manuscript and give honest feedback. Thank you for the genuine joy you've shown as God has opened doors.

Kristen, thank you for holding the reins and making all the hard calls while I have been out of pocket. You have lifted a ridiculous amount of weight off my shoulders. Thank you for loving and believing in me.

All the Guarded Leading Ladies—you know who you are! Guarded is what it is today because of your constant love, support, and hard work. Thank you for letting me share your stories with the world. God is glorified in your lives and will continue to use you to change others. For those whose stories I wasn't able to share, stay tuned for book #2.

Julia Noe, thank you for taking the time to write your story. You're an overcomer.

Jocelyn Graham, you amaze me. I will read your books one day. Thank you for sharing your heart with conviction.

To all my amazing family who put up with the long nights and days with my nose in a computer—thank you for extending grace and encouragement.

Angie Williams, Dominga McCarroll, Susanna Jarvis, and Tammy Combs—thank you for being my prayer partners. Your love, prayers, direction, and encouragement make me a better person, pastor, and leader, but the best part is you make me a better follower of Jesus.

Dr. Sam Chand—thank you for your guidance and investment in my life. None of it has been wasted on me.

Avail Publishing Team—Thank you for your investment into *Guarded*. It has been an honor to work with each of you!

FOREWORD

As you drive through neighborhoods, you'll see signs in some yards saying "Guarded By" followed by the name of a company. That doesn't mean that an armed guard is guarding the property. It does mean that systems have been installed on the property to alert the owners of any extraordinary incident that might even inform the police or other appropriate agencies to respond. Why? Because that property is guarded.

When you were born physically, your parents guarded you. I still recall some major spankings I received because of one repeated infraction. There were some kids in our neighborhood that I was not allowed to play with. Why? Because my parents wanted to guard me from detrimental influences. Of course, as a kid, I had no concept of "bad company," but my guardians guarding me did.

When you are born again and switch your citizenship to heaven and embrace eternal life through Jesus, there's a change of guard. Sin and evil influencers were guarding you from the One who died for us. They did everything within their power to keep you from supernatural transformation and eternal life awaiting us. But when the Spirit invited you, and you accepted His invitation—there was a change of guards. Now, He guards you.

I'm sure my life challenges are the same as yours. My greatest challenge is guarding me from me. Guarding my heart from opportunities that are not His. Guarding my heart from temptations that will destroy me. Guarding my life from destructive relationships. Guarding my thought life, so I sin not against Him and others.

There's a sign in front of your home—your life—and it says, "Guarded by Jesus!"

My friend Pastor Melissa Graham has brought us a most timely yet timeless message:

GUARDED!

Sam Chand
Leadership Consultant and author of VOICES

INTRODUCTION

"Guard your heart above all else, for it determines the course of your life."
—PROVERBS 4:23 (NLT)

Proverbs 4:23 has been a life verse that has guided me since my early teenage years. At first glance, it can be an easily overlooked verse. But anyone who has lived life long enough understands its importance. The words "above all else" should be taken just as they are written. The author wanted to focus on one word: Guard. It was the only verb indicating responsibility for the reader to take action. In other words, as humans, if we care about the course and impact of our lives, we must be "guarded." We lead our lives carelessly without care and intentionality to do this one simple thing. What does it look like to be guarded?

In the vast landscape of human experience, guarded often evokes images of fortresses, barriers, and an instinctive retreat from vulnerability. However, this book invites you to reconsider guarded in a different light—one that intertwines wisdom and purpose. Here, to be guarded is not a mere act of defense or a withdrawal into selfishness but a conscious choice to protect and nurture what is precious within us: our values, relationships, and God's purpose for our lives.

The Word of God reminds us that wisdom is not merely the accumulation of knowledge but the application of insight and discernment given to us by God Himself. It involves knowing when to say yes and when to say no and understanding the balance between openness and self-preservation. In this sense, to be guarded is to be wise. It is to create boundaries that allow us to maintain our core values amidst the chaos and demands of the external world.

Purpose, the compass guiding our actions and decisions, requires clarity and faithfulness. By being guarded, we ensure that our purpose remains untainted and unwavering. We protect our time and energy from distractions and diversions that do not align with our actual goals. In this context, being guarded is not about shutting out the world but about selectively engaging with it in ways that enrich and advance our journey. The book of Proverbs urges the reader to partner with wisdom. A parent pleads to their child to take the life they are given and ensure God's purpose is fulfilled by guarding the heart with wisdom.

This book explores how embracing a guarded mindset can lead to a life of greater fulfillment and authenticity. Through stories, reflections, and practical advice, we will discover the art of setting boundaries, making intentional choices, and cultivating a space where God's best for our lives can flourish. It challenges the notion that guarding is to withhold, suggesting instead that it is a profound act of self-respect and purposeful living.

In *Guarded*, you will discover the transformative power of protecting what matters most, not out of fear but out of a deep conviction for the life you are meant to live. Let this book be a source of encouragement as you navigate the delicate balance between wisdom and purpose and learn to guard your path with purpose-driven intention. A heart and life that are guarded well are life-giving and can't help but be a fountain of life to others.

HEART CENTRAL

"Dear friend, I hope all is well with you and that you are as healthy in body as you are strong in spirit."
—3 JOHN 1:2 (NLT)

Nothing quite took my breath away like the sound of my baby's first heartbeat. I can remember the first appointment as if it were yesterday. The day had finally come. Excitedly, we strolled into the doctor's office with so many questions. Calm yet giddy, feeling like something significant was in store, but clueless as to what was about to happen. This day, a medical doctor would confirm what the home test revealed—a viable pregnancy. I recall sitting on the table, waiting for confirmation to silence the doubt. I had no idea what to expect. I remember holding my breath as the nurse carefully placed the Doppler machine on my belly. Then it happened! Suddenly, the random swishing sound was replaced by a solid rhythmic beat. The nurse confirmed what I assumed. "That's your baby's heartbeat," she said. It was that moment. That sound changed everything for me.

I've heard it said, "A picture is worth a thousand words." The sound sent a thousand thoughts swirling through my mind at that moment. Over the next nine months, I had so much to learn about myself, pregnancy, and the baby. But I would never have to be taught the magnitude of what was inside of my womb. A beating heart. This little life was drawing life from mine. My heart was beating in tandem with hers. For the first time in my life, I had come face to face with the undeniable value of my heart. My heart was giving life to another human other than myself. What a weight, what a responsibility. My heart had to be strong. Another heart now depended on mine for survival.

> *Your heart is the epicenter of your life.*

This simple truth has much more meaning to me now than it did at that moment. Your heart is central to life. It is central to your physical well-being. It is central to your spiritual and emotional well-being. Your heart is the epicenter of your life. In other words, your heart is the center focus of life. The starting point. As your heart goes, so goes your body. Heart health determines life strength. There are no shortcuts. It's God's miraculous design. Its importance cannot be overstated. Your heart powers your life. Therefore, your heart holds the power to your purpose. Your physical, emotional, and spiritual existence relies on your heart.

FACTS ABOUT YOUR PHYSICAL HEART

The heart is a powerful organ comprising muscle and tissue. The heart sits just behind the rib cage in the front left-center of your body. It powers the human body, like electricity powers your home. The National Heart, Lung, and Blood Institute shares how the heart pumps:

> *Electrical signals cause muscles to contract. Your heart has a special electrical system called the cardiac conduction*

system. This system controls the rate and rhythm of the heartbeat. With each heartbeat, an electrical signal travels from the top of the heart to the bottom. As the signal travels, it causes the heart to contract and pump blood.[1]

The heart is responsible for pumping blood through the entire human body. Blood leaves the heart through arteries, which transport oxygen and nutrients to all the major organs. Once the oxygen and nutrients are gone, the blood picks up carbon dioxide and waste and travels back toward the lungs and heart through veins. Once the carbon dioxide is gone, we exhale it. The process then repeats itself with every heartbeat.[2] Our bodies are miraculous. Have you ever stopped to think about all the vital organs inside your body that you need to work well to live? Without the heart, none would be healthy. Everything about your life depends on your heart to have the health and strength needed to do its job. God designed the human body with such care and detail.

HEART AND BRAIN CONNECTIONS

By now, it's clear that the heart is central to the health of your body. But without the brain and heart connected, a person doesn't live in a functional emotional and physical state. The British Heart Foundation explains the connection of the heart to the brain scientifically:

The autonomic nervous system controls many of the body's functions—pretty much anything that our body does without us having to think about it, such as sweating, digestion, or the blood pressure in our arteries. One part of the autonomic nervous system is the vagus nerves, which run up either side of the neck. These nerves connect the brain with some of our

---

[1] "How the Heart Beats," *National Heart Lung and Blood Institute*, accessed May 1, 2024, https://www.nhlbi.nih.gov/health/heart/heart-beats.

[2] "In Brief: How Does the Blood Circulatory System Work?" *InformedHealth.org* [Internet], 21 Nov. 2023, https://www.ncbi.nlm.nih.gov/books/NBK279250/#:~:text=The%20blood%20circulatory%20system%20(cardiovascular,it%20back%20to%20the%20heart.

internal organs, including the heart. They allow the brain to receive information about how hard the heart works and send commands to control how quickly it beats.

The heart and the brain are in constant communication. The communication is not one-sided. The heart feels the emotions processed by the brain, causing our heart to beat faster or slower due to a chemical reaction of oxytocin. During emotional distress or heartbreak, our hearts can physically feel the pain of emotion. "When it comes to our hearts and keeping them healthy, the role of the brain is often forgotten," says Professor Gourine.[3] God, our Creator, took so much time on us. He ensured our intricate design would be full of beautiful partnerships.

We must ensure they are running top-notch if we want to live long and healthy lives. We just read that the heart powers the entire body. If our hearts aren't healthy, our brains and thinking will not be healthy. Our organs all draw their nutrients from what the heart sends. Our breathing, inhalation, and exhalation are dependent on our heart. If the heart is struggling, so is the brain. In other words, what is healthy for your heart is healthy for your brain. Lifespan Cardiovascular Wellness and Prevention Center describes it this way:

Dr. Tina Burton, vascular neurologist *with Lifespan, says, "Our heart and brain are tightly linked. A healthy heart translates to a healthy brain," [and] Dr. Wen-Chih (Hank) Wu . . . cardiologist and director says, "Both the heart and the brain share vascular risk factors, so what's good for your blood vessels are good for both the heart and the brain."*[4]

---

3 "Is the Heart Connected to the Brain?," *British Health Foundation,* accessed April 17, 2024, https://www.bhf.org.uk/informationsupport/heart-matters-magazine/research/is-the-heart-connected-to-the-brain#:~:text=One%20part%20of%20the%20autonomic,internal%20organs%2C%20including%20the%20heart.

4 Lifespan Blog Team et al., "What's Good for Your Heart Is Good for Your Brain," Lifespan, 8 Feb. 2024, https://www.lifespan.org/lifespan-living/whats-good-your-heart-good-your-brain#:~:text=Healthy%20Heart%20and%20Healthy%20Brain%20Tips&text=Those%20steps%20include%20managing%20your,important%20role%20in%20your%20health.

heart to brain communication
THE HEART COMMUNICATES TO BRAIN MORE THAN VICE VERSA

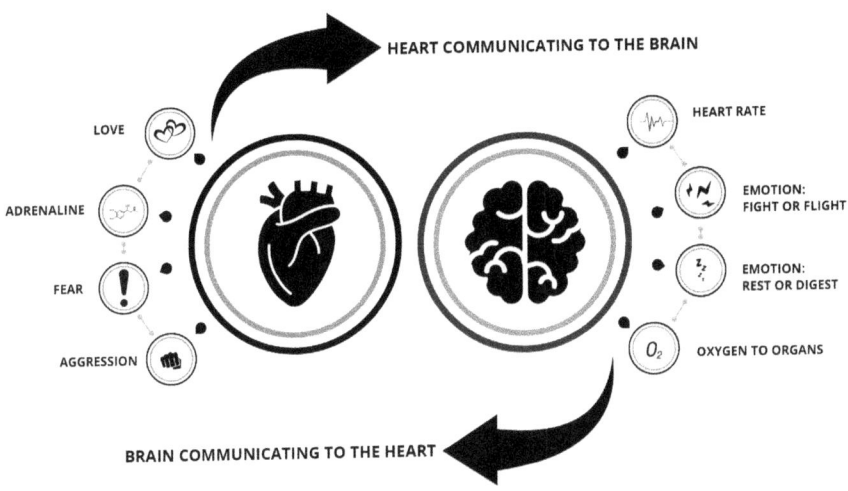

All the sources above suggest that the heart sends more information to the brain than the brain sends to the heart. One will always affect the other. Science and Scripture come together in such a powerful way. The bottom line is that our heart health is imperative. Being in great physical shape means our hearts are strong and healthy. Our brains, major organs, and entire body depend on our heart to do its job daily! If the heart has this much power, we should focus on its health.

A CHANGE IN LIFESTYLE

Maybe it is because I have crossed the forty-year mark, but I have become highly interested in the wellness of my heart and mind. After receiving blood tests that I wasn't happy with, I sought help. Over the last year, I have met with a Health and Digestive Coach. Regularly, we meet to discuss how I can change the unhealthy patterns I created. Those unhealthy patterns were affecting my health significantly. When you are younger, you don't always consider how your choices affect your whole body. At least I didn't. What we put in fuels our body and creates the energy our heart runs on.

In January 2023, during our church's twenty-one days of prayer and fasting, the Lord began to deal with my heart about health. My husband and I had just celebrated our twentieth year in full-time ministry. We were setting our sights on taking a sabbatical that coming summer, something we had never done. We had committed to a mentor, and we would make it a priority. If you have never heard that term used, it means a time of rest. For us, it meant taking an extended time away from the church—a time for fun to refresh our family and marriage. We also chose to take intentional time during that sabbatical to be in solitude with the Lord. This time would allow us to step away from the stress of doing ministry and carrying the weight on our shoulders to hear from the Lord.

If you have ever served in full-time ministry or a profession where you can never turn it "off" or clock out, you understand. We were so excited! Stepping away in this manner would require months of planning and communication to ensure all responsibilities were covered. I am the type A when it comes to making a plan and executing that plan. The thought of being a burden to anyone and needing to know everything is covered causes me to overplan. Overplanning is a trait that has served me well but also drives me crazy, lol.

By January, the plan for July was almost complete. I knew a lot had to be done leading up to our getaway. I wanted to ensure we could really be "gone." So many people would carry extra weight to help us rest. We have the best team of staff and leaders in the world. Thankfully, they made it so easy to go. By the time prayer and fasting arrived in January of that year, I was proud of us for choosing to take a sabbatical. All the planning allowed me to dream and truly participate without stress. I even began to lose the anxious thoughts about what could happen while we were away. The excitement was mounting!

Around day eleven of prayer and fasting, the Holy Spirit began to deal with my heart. By "deal," I mean He started putting His finger on an area that needed my attention and didn't let it go.

My mindset is sometimes unrealistically optimistic; the glass is always half-full for me. Anytime things get too serious, I find myself cracking a joke or making a statement to lighten the weight of the moment. Day eleven was NOT one of those times. I had no reply when the Holy Spirit spoke to me that day. I was on my face at 6 a.m. at the altar, asking God to search me. "If there is anything in my life that isn't pleasing to you, God, show me so I can make it right," I said. And that is just what He did. He spoke to my heart.

When I hear the Holy Spirit speak to me, it is usually not audible; it's a conversation in my spirit. It is overwhelming to know that what is going through your heart and mind at that moment is not you. He is the voice that John 10:27 (ESV) speaks of when he says, "My sheep hear My voice, and I know them, and they follow me." Jesus had to leave the earth so that the Holy Spirit, the third person of the Godhead, could come and fill believers. That same Holy Spirit is here to empower the church to live with boldness so that God's purpose can be fulfilled on earth. He is always speaking; it is our job to listen. Paul tells the church that the Spirit of God speaks in Hebrews 3:15 (ESV): "Today, if you hear His voice, do not harden your hearts." If He is speaking, I want to listen. He will only speak things that guide me closer to Him and His purpose.

The word He spoke to me was *discipline*. That, in and of itself, isn't too bad; what I knew was coming behind it made me nervous. God had my full attention at that moment as I felt the loving rebuke of the Father coupled with an invitation: *You work hard to discipline your spirit, emotions, and the work I have called you to. But what about your body?* Yeah, the feeling I got in the pit of my stomach was nausea. I know Him well enough to know that He never asks a question to which He doesn't already know the answer. He asks a question, so YOU will discover the answer to it.

I know what the Word of God says about it in 1 Corinthians 6:19-20 (NLT):

> *"Don't you realize that your body is the temple of the Holy Spirit, who lives in you and was given to you by God? You do not belong to yourself, for God bought you with a high price. So you must honor God with your body."*

If our physical bodies aren't healthy, we will limit our effectiveness in the Kingdom of God. I knew He was not just talking about weight; that was only a piece of the puzzle. For starters, honoring your physical man means water intake, food, exercise, sleep, managing stress, ensuring that you have the right vitamins, and knowing what's in your blood and what isn't—the list goes on.

> *Denial doesn't change the truth; it only prolongs the problem.*

My first thought was, *Lord, can we just let this one slide? Lord, don't you know how much is on my shoulders? I don't have time to go to the gym and plan healthy meals. I stay up working because there is so much I need to do for You. I am giving my all for You in ministry so others can make it to heaven. Don't You have any quick fixes You could zap me with to make me healthy?* I am so thankful for a patient Father who understands that we are human and who gives us grace *because* we are human. At the end of all my denial and reasoning, He was there waiting.

Denial doesn't change the truth; it only prolongs the problem. That is what was happening in my life. Denial was more manageable than focusing on reality. I was physically fit until my mid-twenties. Somewhere between life, ministry, higher education, work, and having kids, I had allowed my physical body to be at the end of the line. I would go through seasons where I would do great, and then my routine would get highjacked. It took me until now to accept that I struggled in this area—I knew it had to be addressed. Denial had built a space of comfort. The only way out of a place in which we have grown comfortable is to completely shift into discomfort. I don't know if you're like me, but I am an all-or-nothing kind of girl. I'm either in or out. For the last fifteen years of my life, if I couldn't do it with all my daily efforts, I didn't do it at all. I would go through seasons of trying, but one day of failure was enough to stop me for months. My heart would tell my head, "You won't be able to do this." I would allow excuses to rob me of progress.

I argued with the Lord for the rest of my prayer time. I felt sorry for myself, and I got angry at myself for getting angry. I tried to justify my physical negligence. It's not like I was as bad as others; there are so many who do so much worse. After all, I live my life to help others. Wasn't it selfish to prioritize me? At the end of every excuse, I felt the redeeming love of Jesus inviting me deeper into discipline.

By day twelve, I was done making excuses. I had run out of reasons to stay in my emotions and reasoning. I was ready to repent and surrender. So, I responded, *Yes, Lord, I accept Your correction. Forgive me. Please help me do everything I can naturally and give me strength beyond what I feel I have to get to where I need to be. Please give me the strength to live this discipline for the rest of my life. On days of failure, please remind me of grace. And when I succeed, receive it as worship.* And then it all began.

I told you I am a crazy planner. Physical discipline, like any discipline, would take a plan to succeed. I started listing what I needed to do to prepare for a life change. The list was long. But I decided to take it one day at a time. After all, it took me fifteen years to get to this place. Weight was part of the change. Carrying around excess weight isn't healthy for your heart. I will touch on that more. I needed to get blood work done to see what was going on inside my body. A change in my diet, increased regular exercise, proper nutrition through added vitamins and supplements, and more sleep were all at the top of my list. The journey began! If our hearts are going to be healthy, we have to take care of them. Our physical heart matters to the Lord. Our spiritual and emotional hearts matter to Him as well. Heart health only comes through an intentional decision.

When our physical bodies aren't healthy, we will limit our effectiveness for the Kingdom of God. I will share more about this journey throughout our time together. For this moment, I need you to understand this: He created us and has a purpose for us to fulfill. We must be willing to allow Him to show us any area of our lives that needs to change. Especially those areas that are hard for us to acknowledge. If compromise is present in any area of our lives, then our life is weakened, and we are at greater risk of allowing the wrong things into our hearts.

> *Our whole existence is tied to the health of our hearts: physically, spiritually, and emotionally.*

All my life, I have heard it said, "The definition of insanity is doing the same things over and over again and expecting to get different results." (This is true in any area of our lives.) When we allow God to put His finger on the places that need to be changed and respond to change them, we invite the supernatural to happen! We have to decide that our hearts are worth the effort. Our whole existence is tied to the health of our hearts: physically, spiritually, and emotionally.

MAKING THE CONNECTION

Hopefully, you have learned some cool facts about the heart by now. If you love science and the human body, this may have been right up your alley. There is so much depth to the connection between the heart and mind. If what we have discussed so far hasn't hit home for you or has triggered emotions you weren't ready for, don't give up. We are in this together. With our hearts, everything is connected. I want to bring some thoughts full circle to set up what is coming. We serve a God that connects all things. Connectivity and detail that point back to Him are found throughout our bodies. Genesis 1:26-27 tells us we were made in His image, which means we are connected to our Creator in the same manner.

God the Father in Genesis converses with God the Son and the Holy Spirit. We know that the Holy Spirit was there because in Genesis 1:2, as God is creating the heavens and the earth, verse 2 says that the Spirit was hovering over the face of the waters. So, the Father is having a conversation with His Son and Spirit. In Genesis 1:26 (ESV), He says, "Let us make man in our image." What is that image? It is flesh and spirit and heaven and earth put together in one being—all for the glory of the Father, Son, and Holy Spirit. We're divinely created; this is essential to understanding God's purpose for our hearts. The parallels between our physical heart and our eternal heart are so easy to connect.

We are human flesh with an expiration date. We are also souls created for eternity—our souls, designed to bear God's image. In the beginning, before sin entered the garden, the soul of humanity was made perfectly. Ecclesiastes 7:29 says, "This only have I found: God created mankind upright, but they have gone in search of many schemes." God's creation in Adam and Eve was perfection. It was mankind's free will that became their downfall. They weren't aware yet that their disobedience would take their freedom.

Because the serpent was deceptive, he was able to turn Eve's heart to question the words of her Creator. The serpent convinced them. Their hearts knew better. God told them to stay away from the tree of the knowledge of good and evil. He gave them the entire garden but this one tree He said, "Don't eat from it or you will surely die" (Genesis 2:17, author paraphrase). Jeremiah 17:4 tells us that the human heart is the most deceptive and wicked thing of all. Deception, when it's fully grown, gives birth to sin. Sin took this perfect place of eternal communion with our Creator and brought destruction and death. When sin entered, death became imminent. Sin cut our connection to the Creator. The heart is now flawed, temporary, broken, and needing redemption. Even in sin, God had a plan.

Jesus is the plan. He was crucified. He shed His precious blood. His death and resurrection brought back our freedom. He gave His heart to pay the ransom for ours, and because He paid the price, salvation is a gift to ANYONE who believes. What a plan. What LOVE!!!! What a Savior! The concept is almost more than our human minds can conceive. He conquered sin, deception, and death. He paid the price so our hearts could connect with our Creator again. When we put our hope and faith in Jesus, that freedom is ours. We are born again into a new life. We get a new heart. Understand this: For our salvation, Jesus gave us everything. It cost us nothing. Salvation is His gift to all of humanity. Past, present, and future, we now have hope. But keeping our hearts free and connected to Him will cost us everything. It is our response to His sacrifice. Our response is what Matthew 16:24 means when it says to take up our cross, deny ourselves, and follow Him. Creation responds to our Creator by guarding the gift of a redeemed heart. Jesus did all the work to buy back our hearts, and our job for the rest of our days is to do all the work to ensure its safekeeping because this physical life is not the end. We will breathe our last here on this earth with our physical bodies, or we will leave this temporary world when He returns.

He promised in His Word that He will return (see Acts 1:11). When Christ returns, He is coming back for the hearts that have accepted His gift of salvation. All we will have to return to Him is our hearts. It will be an act of worship that we give back to Him on that day. The new heart He paid for with His blood powers the life of our spirit man. That's our eternal being. Once we receive this gift, our entire lives will be different. No matter your heart's condition, I am honored you are here. I need to ask you the most critical question you will ever answer: What kind of condition is your heart in today? *Have you accepted the gift of a new heart through salvation in Jesus?* Where is the health of your heart today? You may have already put your faith and hope in Jesus Christ. If so, that's amazing; I am so proud of you. If reading this puts you at a crossroads because you have not yet accepted Jesus into your heart, you are in the right place. I want to lead you to Jesus! Maybe you have had a relationship with Him but are entirely disconnected from your Creator. It's time to reconnect. Everything could change for you in one moment. You can start over. Life can be different. He has a new heart ready to give you if your heart is tired, hurting, broken, lifeless, or sick.

Surrender is a shame-free zone. This moment is going to change everything. Allow me the honor of walking you through the most significant decision you will ever make—giving your heart to Jesus. Your heavenly Father loves YOU so much. That is why He sent His only Son to die in your place (see John 3:16). Take a deep breath. Awaken to the beat of your Creator's heart. Let your rhythm sync with His. He will make you new. Allow His love to change you.

> **If you want to make Jesus the Lord of your life, pray this short prayer:**
>
> *"Heavenly Father, I come to You in the name of your Son, Jesus. Thank You for sending Your Son to take my place and die for my sins. I admit I am a sinner in need of a Savior. I believe that You are the one true God, the Creator of my heart. I accept the gift of salvation and profess You as the Lord of my life. Take my old heart and give me a new heart. I will spend the rest of my days guarding the heart You have given me. Please help me to grow in Your Word and in the knowledge of who You are. I ask all this in Jesus's name, AMEN!"*

If you prayed that prayer from your heart, all of heaven rejoiced! *Take a moment to close your eyes and thank Him for what He has done.* Talk to God like you are talking to a friend. He knows you. He sees you. He has made you new! The prayer is the beginning of walking into a new life in Christ. The prayer was the easy part. The rest is up to you. Find a good Bible-believing church near you and get connected. It would be best to go somewhere where you can have people walk alongside you as you grow in your faith.

If you live in East Tennessee, I welcome you to join us at The Avenue Church in Morristown, Tennessee. If you are too far to attend in person, we would love to have you join us online. You can catch our services live on Sundays at www.theavenuemorristown.com or check out our YouTube channel, @theavenuemorristown. If you are connected to a church, make sure you tell someone about your new commitment to Christ. The Kingdom of God is a family; one day, we will be together in heaven, so let someone celebrate this decision with you. If you want to share it with me, I would love to rejoice! You can send an email to info@melissagraham.org.

HEARTBEAT

Everything changes when we die to our old lives and put our faith in Jesus. Our next step is to learn how to care for the new heart inside us. Our heart now beats for our Creator. Our lives should move more towards His likeness every day. Less of us, more of Him. Why? So that His will for our lives is clear to see. He has plans for you; He made that clear in Jeremiah 29:11. Those plans He has for you are good and not evil. He knows where you have been, where you are, and where you are going. You can trust Him. He will get you to the destination of your purpose. He created the map.

How can we show God that we are committed to guarding our hearts? I have the best news. It doesn't matter if you are a Bible scholar or on day one of the journey of learning His Word. You guard your heart the same way you walk with your Creator: one day at a time. Let God know you depend on Him. You need Him. You are desperate for Him to lead you. He already knows, but acknowledging it shifts your focus like a child dependent on your parent to provide everything you need. That is how we should depend on our heavenly Father.

When my son was born, he had difficulty breathing outside of the womb. The doctors called his respiratory problem a transition delay. Transitional delay describes the distress of a newborn who struggles to adjust and needs to learn how to breathe oxygen. They noticed the delay within minutes after his birth. When they took him out of my arms to get him to the NICU, it was one of the worst moments in my life. The little one that I had carried for the last eight and a half months was taken from me. Nurses told me it was a common issue for newborns, so I tried to calm my mind.

The medical team proceeded to share that the acclimation process would be more successful if I could hold him against my heart. Until that moment, it never dawned on me that my heart was his comfort because he had been connected to me in the womb. Now, he was in a great big world. Separated, he could no longer hear my heartbeat, and he felt lost. I got to him as soon as I was able. They were right. When I placed his precious little ear against my chest, he immediately knew who was holding him. His breathing settled, and his tense little body melted into mine. He was quiet as if to listen. My heart was his favorite song. He knew he was back where he needed to be.

That is what our heavenly Father's heart does for us. In comparison, we cannot physically hear His heart. Our spirit hears, and we are captivated immediately like a smell that brings back a memory or a song that evokes tears of days gone by. Salvation reconnects us with His heartbeat. It's a sound our hearts know. We were made in His image. He is our Creator. We belong to Him, no matter what has happened in our lives or where our journey has taken us. No matter what we have been through, we know His heart. The steady rhythm brings peace. It fills us with joy. Our heart settles in His presence. We know everything is going to be okay.

It is now a choice to allow the rhythm of His heart to set the rhythm of our own. Remember, after salvation, the rest is on us. Choose to do the work. Make the hard choices. Keep the right people in your lives and the wrong people out. Grow to know His will for your life. Get His Word in your heart so you know how to keep sin out—by filling your heart with more of Him and less of the world. Allow Him to hold you close and find protection there. Choose to allow His heart to heal any wounds of your past. Lastly, allow Him to lead you confidently into your future.

My son's time in the NICU was brief, but because I was there, he didn't know he wasn't home. My presence made his healing easy. He is my baby. I would never leave him. The hospital gave me a room so that I could be there 24/7 to rock him, feed him, and sing to him. He went through painful procedures. I could not stop the pain, but in those moments, his hands were wrapped in mine, making the pain bearable. My voice kept his attention and made the hard things easier.

God's presence in our lives is the same. He is always present. We are His. There is no way He will ever leave us on this journey. When we stay close to Him, we can walk through anything. The peace in His presence calms our fears. And when we walk through times of pain, we can rest knowing we are wrapped in His arms, against His chest, memorizing the rhythm of His heart. Our responsibility in the equation is to keep our hearts close to His daily.

PRAYER OF COMMITMENT

Father, you are the Creator of my heart. I know that my heart is what You want. Thank You for sending Your son to pay the price to buy back what sin stole. It is my desire to be close to You and have a heart that beats like Yours. I know that You care about my mind, body, and soul. Help me to take my heart as seriously as You do in all of those ways. In Jesus's name, AMEN.

MY HEART, MY RESPONSIBILITY

*"Create in me a pure heart, O God, and
renew a steadfast spirit within me."*
—PSALM 51:10

It is human nature at times to want to escape responsibility. I can remember watching my children play when they were young. Jocelyn, my daughter, is seventeen months older than my son Judah. Watching them always intrigued me. I loved to see them interact. Every mother's dream is that their children enjoy one another and learn to play and interact in a healthy and productive way. When my kids were young, ages three and four, they hadn't learned to regulate their emotions. Enjoying one another at playtime was a challenge. Jocelyn would have the toy Judah wanted, so He would take it. Jocelyn, in turn, would hit or pinch him to take it back, and he would cry to get our attention.

If you are a parent who has seen this type of interaction between your children, you understand what I am describing. If you are not a parent, know that at that moment, complete pandemonium breaks out. With children, one action results in a response, which results in another response, and so on and so forth. When these scenarios happen, it would not have been helpful to sit them down and explain the problem using adult language. It would be challenging to break down each part of the scenario and talk to them through the scene moment by moment. Their ability to understand was dependent on the maturity of their minds.

I did what I thought a good parent would do. I stopped each of them and held them accountable for their actions. I said something like, "Judah, you are in time out for taking the toy from your sister. You have to learn how to share. When you want to play with something she has, you have to learn to ask or wait your turn," and, "Jocelyn, you are in time out because you responded to one wrong action with another wrong action. You cannot hit your brother. You should have come to us for help."

You may have been in a similar situation. Your idea of discipline may look different. Similar responses could always be expected from my young children. As soon as we held them accountable for their actions, they immediately shifted the blame. Insisting the responsibility to be the fault of their sibling. "She was playing with the toy I wanted and holding it on purpose so I couldn't have it, so I took it," or "He took my toy, so I hit him!" There have been times when my need to escape responsibility caused me to shift blame. No matter the situation, we were attempting to teach our children from a young age that no matter what anyone else does, you are responsible for your own life and actions.

ONE LIFE

We have one life, one opportunity to fulfill our God-given purpose. If we are going to guard and care for our lives as we should, we have to take ownership. We have to do more than just understand how our thoughts and emotions affect our lives. We have to take our knowledge a step further and make it personal! It is our responsibility to discover from where our thoughts and emotions derive.

We are responsible for investigating how they direct our lives. We are responsible for making the necessary changes to ensure our hearts are healthy.

> *My heart is my responsibility. My heart is worth guarding.*

We have to take responsibility for our own hearts! If, at this moment, you're tempted to run because it sounds like more than you bargained for, let me encourage you; you can do this. If you commit to this journey, it will change everything for the better. Taking responsibility will be a journey of discovery, healing, joy, purpose, and freedom. You must decide for yourself that your heart is worth guarding! Are you ready? Read these words out loud: "My heart is my responsibility. My heart is worth guarding. Handling our hearts responsibly begins with our perspective as we gain understanding."

We must view responsibility through the right lens. We must have a perspective that is free from shame, condemnation, or pride. Only through eyes of hope, love, and redemption will our hearts thrive. That lens of perspective is set throughout our lives. Perspective is set by what we have lived, experienced, and learned. Perspective is shaped by the people and places that have influenced our lives. We are all unique. Much like a fingerprint, no two people experience life the same way. We have all experienced good and bad days, days that make us smile and some that we thought would never end. Our families are unique, and our placement in those families is unique, as well.

We serve a God who knows all about us. In fact, scripture tells us in Psalms 139:13 that He knit us together in our mother's womb. All the days of our lives He has seen and known before one of them ever came to be. That same God says we are intentionally and wonderfully made. No matter how good or bad the experiences of our lives have been, He has a plan. We only need to acknowledge it and offer our lives up for His use. He will take care of the plan as we take care of the heart within us.

GROWING IN RESPONSIBILITY

We need to understand responsibility. It isn't such a scary word. Let's define it. *Merriam-Webster's Dictionary* defines it as: "the quality or state of being responsible: such as moral, legal, or mental accountability; reliability, trustworthiness; something for which one is responsible: burden."[5]

You are accountable and expected to guard your heart with wisdom and integrity so that you can accomplish God's purpose in your life.

---

5 *Merriam-Webster Dictionary online,* s.v. "responsibility," accessed January 25, 2024, https://www.merriam-webster.com/dictionary/responsibility#dictionary-entry-1.

So, according to the definition, we could say that you are accountable and expected to guard your heart with wisdom and integrity so that you can accomplish God's purpose in your life. This responsibility is an expected response to Christ's salvation of our hearts. He has redeemed your life. Romans 12 tells us that we are to offer ourselves as "living sacrifices" to God as a reasonable act of worship because our lives don't belong to us; they were bought with a price. We can't know His will for our lives unless we offer them back to Him. He wants us to discover His good, pleasing, and perfect will. When we take responsibility to guard the gift God deposited on the inside of us, we are saying to God: "You paid the price for this heart, so I will honor You by guarding it with everything I have." The stewardship of my heart is the best gift I can return to Him.

Responsibilities . . . we all have them. Our lives are full of things and people we are responsible for daily. Responsibility only increases from adolescence into adulthood; it cannot be avoided. Our families, jobs, extra-curricular activities, bills, volunteer opportunities, and keeping up with all of the amazing people in our lives can take the place of us prioritizing the responsibility we have to ourselves. Either we face up to our responsibilities or suffer the consequences of a life spiraling out of control. We have one life, and the condition of that life is either created by what we allow or by what we choose.

You may have heard that you can't always control what happens to you, but you can control how you respond. As we get older, it is imperative that we learn that lesson. For example, that is why we know we must adhere to the law of the land. We obey speed limits if we like to keep our money from being wasted paying tickets and higher insurance prices. One thing I have come to understand in life is that not all adults know how to be responsible.

If growth in responsibility is going to happen, we must first stop and take inventory of where we are. How responsible are you in your life? Apply this question to any area. Those areas may be relational, emotional, financial, professional, or spiritual. It takes a mature person to be able to inspect your life with honesty. So, let's do it! Take inventory of your life. Please give yourself a score and list why you chose it. Start a positive and negative chart for each area. What do the results of your life in these areas tell you? Are you intentional about the life that you are living in these areas? When you take a close look at them, what do you see?

- Relationships
- Emotional Health
- Financial Stability
- Professional Life
- Physical Body
- Spiritual Well Being

Are you currently taking responsibility for each of those areas? If you are ready for the challenge, it will be all growth from here.

WHY IS MY HEART IN THE SHAPE IT'S IN?

There are several answers to this question, and all must be understood and acknowledged to address your state of mind adequately. The first reason your heart is in the shape it's in is because of the sin in the world.

We discussed the fall in the garden in the last chapter, so we don't need to delve into all the details again. However, some things cannot be overstated. The short and simple answer to the state of the human heart is SIN. Since the fall of man in the Garden of Eden in Genesis 1, humanity has found ways to mess up the state of the human heart. From Genesis 1 to this moment, humanity is born with the need for a Savior. Our lives and hearts are born into sin. They are imperfect and flawed and have needed healing from the very beginning. Our lives are empty. Our emotions are out of balance. Our hearts are cursed because of sin, and we have the wrong perspective. All of this is why we need a new heart.

In other words, we require a heart transplant. How do we attain this? By allowing the love of Christ to fill us. John 3:16-17, maybe the most famous scripture in the Bible, says, "God loved the people of this world so much that he gave his only Son, so that everyone who has faith in him will have eternal life and never really die. God did not send his Son into the world to condemn its people. He sent him to save them!" (CEV) His sacrifice tells us His intentions for us, the world, and fallen humanity. His heart was so strong that it transcended death. He beat hell and conquered the grave. He bought back freedom for the human race, once and for all. If we want this love and His heart to fill our lives, we need only do what Romans 10:10 (NLT) says: "For it is by believing in your heart that you are made right with God, and it is by openly declaring your faith that you are saved." Yes, it is that simple. Why do we make it so complicated?

The day I accepted Christ's love and His forgiveness filled my life for the first time, I was changed. I felt an emotional and physical difference. I was seven years old, and we had been in a Kid's Crusade for three days. This particular night was the final meeting. I can't remember who was in the room, the evangelist's name, or what was said. But I remember my heart racing and hot tears flowing down my face as my heavenly Father knocked on the door of my heart. When it came time for the altar call, I ran to an altar. I hit my knees as if a hurricane-force wind drove me there. I poured my heart out and gave God control of my heart and thirty-six years later, I can tell you—I was changed.

In the days that followed, I remember experiencing so much joy and peace that it's difficult to describe. The same night I experienced salvation, I won the grand prize drawing. I won a basket of toys and treats. I was so full of joy and gratitude that I gave it all to a kid I had noticed in the room all week who never smiled. Trust me, it had to be a real-life change for a seven-year-old to give all their candy away. That was the first time I remember Jesus had completely touched my heart.

> *His love and grace are stronger than any sin wrapped around your heart.*

I wish I could tell you that from that day on, sin was never a problem for me again. I can't because I am still human. I am flesh and spirit, and I had to repent often as I grew. The night of my salvation will forever be etched in my mind. It was the beginning of a relationship with Jesus. That relationship would challenge and change me over and over again. Through the years, I grew in love and relationship with Him. I have learned just how special His love is for me. I've witnessed His grace and mercy in my life. I've experienced how intimate His care for my heart could really be walking through difficult seasons. Through it all, I have learned that the state of my heart is the most critical factor in my life. On the days I failed to protect it as I should, He stood guard faithfully. When I succeeded in protecting my heart as He asked, I felt Him smiling down on me with pride and joy.

His love and grace are stronger than any sin wrapped around your heart. The heaviness of sin was never meant for you to carry. Even right now, in this moment, Jesus is calling your heart, giving you an invitation to run to Him. Bring the shattered pieces of your heart and lay them at His feet. You have felt empty long enough. Mistakes have tormented your mind long enough. He has a new life waiting for you. A heart that is whole and healed from the effects of sin, one that His death and resurrection alone could purchase. All this is available to you, but only you can say "yes" to Jesus and invite Him in. Jesus died to give you freedom, and because He rose again, you can too! It will be a daily choice to stay free from sin. Rise above it and accept His love and forgiveness. Let your heart beat in freedom for the first time in a long time, or maybe for the first time. Nothing you could do is wrong enough to mess it up. It's already been given to you, it's yours if you want it! It is a freedom you can choose to walk in every day.

HEART HISTORY

Mostly, life growing up is full of happy memories! I grew up in a pastor's home. In our house were my mom, dad, and sister, who was seventeen months older. My mom was the kind of mother who would do anything for our family. She was selfless, loving, and full of joy, and she saw the world and her family through pure eyes. She was always, and still is, as pretty as a picture. She always carried herself with such a class. I saw her reading God's Word every day, and I can't remember a time I've seen her worship without tears streaming down her face. I had an amazing dad, full of compassion and godly character, and he always took the time to teach us life lessons in the seemingly mundane moments. He filled our home with laughter and laid a foundation for the kind of man I would choose to marry. Growing up, my daddy was my best friend! He taught me how to ride a bike. He taught me how to shoot a gun. Most importantly, he showed me how to love God and people.

There were years throughout my younger childhood when we didn't have much, but he was always intentional to ensure we didn't feel like we were without. The church he pastored in my elementary years was relatively small, but my dad has never left anything or anyone as he found them. Being around my parents always made anyone or anything better, and it still does. They were to us, as their children, as they are to everyone they meet: **careful with our hearts.** They were loving. They disciplined us so that we would learn lessons that could save us from heartache later in our lives. My parents weren't perfect, but honestly, they were pretty close. In our home, love was never in short supply; family and God were the priority, and serving others was a way of life. Trust and love were the core of my heart's foundation. My heart history was laid firm. Because of this, trust and love were the measuring stick and the lens through which I saw the world.

When you are young, you think everyone's family is like yours. It was not until my high school and college years that I understood that some families were the opposite of mine. Those who experienced differently saw the world entirely differently. In life, our perspective is our reality. We lack the ability early in life to empathize with others. We can see people who are different and do not understand that their reality is very different from ours.

I had a close friend in elementary school that I was around all the time; when you saw one of us, people assumed the other was close in proximity. We loved the same things, played on the same basketball team, attended the same elementary school, and lived in the same community with our families. With all those similarities, the difference in our lives was significant. Her family experience looked so different from mine. Her parents were divorced. Her father battled addiction. His life was unstable, so her relationship with him was minimal. She was bitter and angry at her father. She moved around so much between her mom and grandmother for stability that she ended up in her grandparents' custody. I always enjoyed going to her grandparents' home. They owned a dairy farm, and we always had so many things to keep us busy! Sadly, my family moved from Tennessee to St. Louis, Missouri, when I was in the seventh grade. Our friendship changed—1994 was before social media, email, and cell phones. All we could do was write letters and talk on the phone. By the end of my tenth-grade year, we had grown apart and lost contact.

We eventually reconnected long after college, but our lives looked very different. At that time, I had married my college best friend, and we were in full-time ministry with two fabulous kids. I graduated from Xavier University with a master's degree in counseling and education. My life was at a place where I knew I wanted to spend my life helping others. Around 2009, with social media becoming the norm, I was excited to reconnect with many friends I had lost touch with. One of the first people I looked for was my elementary school friend, and what I discovered broke my heart.

I was shocked to discover she was serving a long sentence in prison for vehicular manslaughter. She had an accident when she was in high school while she was under the influence. How could this happen? She was a great person. She was talented. She was beautiful. All the details I would come to find out left me heartbroken for her. She had begun a life of addiction early in high school, causing her to drop out without finishing. By her early twenties, her addiction was so advanced there wasn't a substance she hadn't tried. She had two kids, so she tried to get clean, but each time, her addiction came back with a vengeance. Her life seemed to be spiraling further out of control. Once out of jail, she was in and out of rehab and treatment facilities. Through the years, I have occasionally watched and kept in touch with her.

Recently, we sat together for the first time in twenty-seven years and shared lunch. My friend shared details about her life and what had happened. In 2023, she gave her life to Jesus for the first time! She had attended church for sixteen years as a child and never had a personal relationship with Jesus. I am happy to share that she has been clean for two years, and we are still in touch. She wants to spend the rest of her life helping others find freedom from where she remained trapped for so long. I am so proud of all the obstacles she has overcome. During our lunch, I asked where her life went wrong. She answered me honestly. Her lifelong bitterness, anger, and heartbreak from the abandonment and pain from her father were deep. He was never there. He couldn't protect her heart because He didn't even value his own. She lived to try and make the pain she felt go away.

The impact our history and family of origin have on our hearts is profound. It's an impact that we don't get to choose but one that we have to acknowledge. If we understand this, we can be aware of the pitfalls that await us due to our upbringing. What does this mean for you? All of us should look at our lives and upbringing. We can try to ignore our heart history, but left unaddressed, it will always come back up in our lives. Somehow and in some way, we have to face our past.

> *God specializes in taking broken things and making them beautiful, all to bring Him glory!*

Once we have entered a relationship with Christ, knowing the truth in His Word is the only way to remain free. That is what we are responsible to do. Why is it harder for some to get there than others? You may have a family that is more like the one I was raised in; if so, that's great! Because of what we have been exposed to in life, we still have to overcome plenty of things. If that is your story, stop now and thank God. If you identify more with my friend's story, you must address it. Guarding our hearts can be incredibly challenging when our upbringing has shown us examples void of hope and truth. What happens when those who have raised us expose us to more than they ever protect us from . . . when our heart history is a place of complete brokenness? Here comes my favorite part! God specializes in taking broken things and making them beautiful, all to bring Him glory!

Bring all the broken pieces of your past to Jesus. He alone can heal us from the heartbreak we never thought we could heal. When Jesus does something, He doesn't do it halfway; we can trust Him as our healer. Psalms 34:18 (NLT) says, "The LORD is close to the brokenhearted; he rescues those whose spirits are crushed." Jesus is no stranger to pain and brokenness. He spent His entire ministry on earth seeking out the hurting and broken. Jesus went after those who didn't have the family examples, those who were sinful, bound, at the end of their rope, and those whose hearts were a total mess!

This is what I love about my Savior. He sees where we are and gave His very life so our family story could be rewritten! Because of the cross, we can have a new family. A new beginning is available. A fresh start is excellent news for us because it means we can have a complete "redo." Because of His precious sacrifice, the shortcomings of the family we know can be washed away. Even Jesus had some interesting characters in His birth family. His family line was full of liars and adulterers; there was even a prostitute and a murderer. Looks like we are in good company to work through some family issues.

When we look at our family history in the light of His Word, we can ask Him to show us what needs healing. What in our lives lines up with His Word, and what is out of place? The reality of the situation is our history has impacted us significantly, some in good ways and others harmful, but we've all been impacted. Our family of origin is the most influential group in our lives because they give us the first lens through which we see life. When we grow and mature, we have to decide if that lens is what we want to use or if we need a new one.

> *We all have a heart history, and we need to identify it and address it appropriately.*

You can be thankful if you grew up in a family that protected your heart and did their best to give you a healthy start in life. Minor changes may need to be made, but if this is your story, you need to stop and thank God. If the story of my friend resonated with you, now is a good time to do some soul-searching. Soul-searching isn't something to enter into lightly. Take some time, get out your Bible, talk to God, and ask Him to show you the areas of your family of origin that have exposed your heart to destruction. Then, wait and listen.

This is the point in your journey where you may need to process with a spouse, trusted friend, or counselor. You cannot and should not walk this road alone, especially if the road is rocky. We all have a heart history, and we need to identify it and address it appropriately. No matter what feelings you have while looking back at your family history, we all have a responsibility to acknowledge and address its impact on our hearts. The history and formative experiences I carry are the vantage points that form the lens through which I see life. In other words, my perspective on life influences my entire life, so we must be all aware of our individual perspectives—what they are and how they impact us today.

THOUGHTS–FEELINGS–CHOICES

THOUGHTS LEAD TO FEELINGS

I believe in the idea that your life will follow your thoughts! I am 100 percent convinced that most, if not all, battles are won or lost in a person's thought life. Show me a person's life, and I can tell you what kind of thought life they have. Actions always follow thoughts. When I was in my master's program at Xavier University studying to become a counselor, we learned a lot about how thoughts affect a person's actions. One of the most important thought patterns is one that, by adulthood, is automatic; it is the subconscious thought.

The term "subconscious mind" was developed to name thought patterns that run unconsciously due to experience and belief. Our perceptions and interpretations come from those beliefs, and those beliefs are then filtered through what has been allowed to stay in our hearts. For example, if a person grows up being told they can do anything and then is raised in an environment where they are allowed the opportunity to achieve great things, then they, in turn, think they can do anything! So, when presented with a problem that needs to be solved, that person's subconscious thoughts give them the lens of, "Of course, you can do this!" They see the problem through because their subconscious thoughts are confident. They face it with optimism and will find a solution to the problem. They will only stop once they succeed!

On the other hand, others are raised believing they are failures and that they will never succeed, and this belief creates a lens through which they can see things. When someone brings them a problem, their viewpoint is pessimistic. Solving a problem could be difficult for them and lead to never overcoming the challenge. The subconscious thoughts begin with the lens of low self-esteem and fear. They are defeated before they even begin. Our beliefs create a lens that shapes our thoughts and drives our feelings. The most important stories are the ones we tell ourselves. They are the script we live by and ultimately cause us to take action that coincides with these two areas: thoughts and feelings.

While in school, counseling theories was one of our course requirements. There is a wide range of theories regarding the best approaches to professional counseling. One that resonates with me the most is cognitive behavioral therapy (CBT). This approach helps people learn how to identify and change destructive or disturbing thought patterns that negatively influence their behavior and emotions. CBT combines cognitive therapy with behavior therapy by identifying maladaptive patterns of thinking, emotional responses, or behaviors and replacing them with more desirable patterns. CBT focuses on changing the automatic negative thoughts that can contribute to and worsen our emotional difficulties, depression, and anxiety. These spontaneous negative thoughts also have a detrimental influence on our mood. Through CBT, a person identifies faulty thoughts and challenges and replaces them with more objective, realistic thoughts.[6] One of the reasons I love counseling so much

---

6 Kendra Cherry, "How Cognitive Behavior Therapy Works," *Verywell Mind,* 2 Nov. 2023, https://www.verywellmind.com/what-is-cognitive-behavior-therapy-2795747.

is because I am fascinated with how the brain works. I know the power that our thought lives hold.

Our hearts give a home to our thoughts and feelings. Once we have allowed thoughts in our hearts to stay, they take root and set up camp. The outcome of those thoughts that have taken root will always be seen through our behavior. The thoughts we think and the opinions we form about ourselves and the world around us are extremely important. Your thought life is powerful. Your thoughts have shaped your decisions and, as a result, your life!

Allow me to share with you an example. As I write this, my son Judah is now sixteen, incredibly handsome, witty, and quite the character. Judah has always had a very strong will. We noticed it right after he was born. Remember the story—he fought to stay in my womb because he didn't want to breathe the air outside. That landed him in the NICU for nine days before finally giving in and adjusting to the real world. Through his toddler years, he was large and in charge. He was not afraid to challenge authority or cross the boundaries. After we parented him into his mid-elementary school years, I thought we had seen all sides of this strong will. We were those parents reading all the books James Dobson had ever written on the strong-willed child because we were fascinated with how strong he was. Basically, when someone tells you they have a strong-willed child, what they are saying is to WATCH OUT when that child makes up their mind about anything.

At age nine, the day came for Judah to get spacers in the top and bottom of his mouth. The purpose of the hardware was to expand his pallet and make room for braces so that he wouldn't have to have permanent teeth pulled. The thing about strong-willed children is they process thoughts from a place of confidence when things are within their control. Thinking through a situation outside of those parameters will produce a very different outcome. Eating and talking feel much different when spacers are placed in your mouth. The pediatric dentist assured us that after a week, all the children she had ever seen at her practice began to eat normally and learned to cope with the devices that were now permanently a part of their mouths. That is until they met Judah. Judah wore those spacers for six months, and at each of his monthly dentist appointments, he astounded the staff at the dentist's office. Judah survived daily on protein shakes, applesauce, yogurt, and runny mashed potatoes! He had made up his mind that he wasn't going to eat because if he did, he would choke on the food. When Judah made up his mind, his behavior always followed his thoughts.

Believe me, as his parents, we begged, disciplined, bribed, prayed, and even put stacks of cash and toys in front of his face to try and get him to eat. All our attempts were futile. We did not feed him any solid food because his mind was more powerful than anything we tried! I am happy to tell you that they removed those right before Thanksgiving; to this day, he has no problem eating solid food! I share that story to show you the power of our thoughts and our belief in those thoughts! Judah's thoughts were powerful; they created his emotions about the whole situation which in turn caused him to act on those emotions.

For some of you reading this today, you have lived years with thoughts and beliefs that have created real emotions and feelings. Those feelings have been fostered through an unhealthy lens or perspective. They cannot be trusted. When those thoughts are not under the Lordship of Jesus, you will always make the wrong choices based on the feelings that come from those thoughts.

You can be free from these false beliefs by weighing every thought by the truth of God's Word. The Bible can cut and divide truth from lies. That is why Romans 12:2 says we should not conform to the thought patterns of this world, but we need the power of God's truth to transform our thinking so that our minds are renewed in truth. Only then will we be able to honestly know what the will of God is for our lives.

On any given day, a person can be bombarded with thousands of thoughts. The only way we will discover if a thought is truth or a lie is to measure it against the Word of God. A lie believed to be true will create a clouded and false lens. A truth believed to be true will create a clear lens. Regardless of its category, belief in thought is the only thing that can form a lens. That lens determines how clearly you see, what you see, or if you see at all.

I wear contacts; without them, everything further than twelve inches from my face is blurry and distorted. My vision problems came on early in life, and I will never forget the first time I was given glasses in elementary school. Suddenly, the world looked so different. I had been walking around for several years, not knowing that the world others saw and the world I saw were different. Before the eye doctor gave me glasses, I thought everyone saw the world the way I saw it. After being given corrected lenses, I saw everything as it should be!

Here's what I am getting at: whatever lens a person is looking through becomes their reality. That's how powerful our perception and thought life is. It can create our lives. I could get on a soap box here if I let myself. The enemy of our souls loves to speak lies to us. He has been doing it from the beginning of time since the Garden of Eden, with Adam and Eve, and he continues it to this day in my heart and in yours. If Satan can get us to believe a lie, we have made his job easy. Our belief in the lie will do far more damage in our hands than he could ever do with his. We will live out the life we see.

> *Lies are destroyed when truth is introduced.*

....

As a pastor, I have seen belief in lies ravage individual lives, marriages, and entire families. If only we would train our hearts to stop in the moment and compare our thoughts to the Word of God. Then, lies wouldn't stay long enough to become planted and grow into belief. Lies are destroyed when truth is introduced. Truth dispels all the false voices because the source of all truth is Christ. Even right now as you read this, I believe that the Holy Spirit is showing you how to discern truth from a lie. The thoughts you've allowed to become beliefs that have tainted your life will be exposed. Anything exposed to the light can no longer be hidden!

Take a moment and pray, and ask the Lord to show you any lies you have accepted as truth! Break free from those by using the Word of God to cut and divide them out of your life. Replace the lie with God's truth for you!

Hopefully, by now, you see just how important and powerful your thought life is to your success. All of us must take responsibility for our thoughts if we want to see our lives grow in a positive direction. If our thoughts aren't measured by what the Word of God says, our actions will be distorted by the world around us. That is a recipe for disaster.

MY CHOICES

We make choices every day. *Harvard Business Review* found the following:

> Various sources suggest that the average adult makes 33,000 to 35,000 total decisions each day, including what we will

eat, what we will wear, what we will say, and how we'll say it. These happen automatically and simultaneously through the information we've subconsciously stored about what is "good" or "bad." Gerald Zaltman, a Harvard Business School professor, suggests that 95% of our cognition occurs in the subconscious mind. This is by necessity—our brains would short-circuit if we had to weigh more than 30,000 decisions one by one.[7]

Those numbers may seem like a lot to you, but anyone who is living and breathing will have to make choices every single day. We make those choices based on the direction of our thoughts. Our thoughts determine and create the boundaries of our actions. It's no surprise that the world around us is acting in ways that are unhealthy and unproductive. Unhealthy thoughts lead to unhealthy actions, just as healthy thoughts lead to healthy actions.

Take a moment now to think about your life choices. Those choices vacillate between wise and not-so-wise at different points in your life based on maturity, stage of life, and emotional health. One thing we will never escape no matter what stage of life we are in is that our choices = our lives. As we have discussed previously, many things can influence those choices. Once you know better, doing better should be the byproduct. I remember times when my thinking and decision-making were mature. As a result of living at that level, I lived out the consequences of choices made at that level. If we want to experience a favorable outcome in life, we have to take the responsibility of our hearts seriously.

---

7   Amanda Reill, "A Simple Way to Make Better Decisions," *Harvard Business Review*, 6 Dec. 2023, https://hbr.org/2023/12/a-simple-way-to-make-better-decisions#:~:text=Various%20sources%20suggest%20that%20the,how%20we'll%20say%20it.

OUR THOUGHTS CREATE OUR FEELINGS AND OUR FEELINGS STEER OUR CHOICES.

KNOWING AND DOING

By now, you get the point. Everything we have discussed leads back to one thing—personal responsibility. It starts with taking responsibility and choosing to examine all the areas we have addressed thus far. Knowing and doing are very different. My goal is to make you better and make you iron, which sharpens you to think and pursue better things! Your heart is so valuable because your life has a specific purpose. For that purpose, no one can live for you. Your Creator has given you a specific purpose for you to accomplish. All of us have work to do. Each day has a purpose.

We are walking towards the purpose and calling God has given us. When we take responsibility for our hearts, we acknowledge and carefully consider the thoughts and feelings that have led us. It means taking ownership of the direction of our lives—standing in the "gate," so to speak! We have power over what we allow in and out of our hearts. We have the authority to make the necessary changes to have the kind of lives we know are available to us! We want a life of fullness, joy, purpose, and growth! The only thing standing between that life and your current one is YOU making the change! When you know better, you should do better. What are you going to do about it? There are only two responses: make excuses or make it happen.

EXCUSES VS. EXPLANATION

We know what needs to change. So, what keeps us from jumping in and taking the reins? Why do excellent intentions often fail to translate into action? Good questions, right? Excuses frequently block the bridge between knowing and doing. You may be thinking, *Sometimes there's a reason. Sometimes, some facts prevent me from passing over the bridge.* And I would tell you, you are right. A factual reason is an explanation. But there is a distinct difference between an explanation and an excuse.

An excuse is most commonly used as a wall to protect someone when they feel attacked. Feelings of shame, guilt, or an attempt to shift blame can cause a person to become defensive. As a result, an excuse is a method of self-preservation and protection. Excuses are used to avoid personal responsibility.[8]

An explanation is a way to clarify the situation. It is less emotional in nature, built on facts, and not emotionally driven. Explanations make way for responsibility to be acknowledged. They bring clarity and understanding so a resolution can happen. Explanations are given when someone wants to be understood. Explanations and excuses are sometimes similar in nature. The only person who knows the difference is the one making them.

Let me give you an example to explain my point. We have two teenagers who drive. In our home, there is a rule. The gas tank has to stay above a quarter of a tank at all times. If it falls below that, they risk being grounded from their car. Let's say one day I move my daughter's car and discover the gauge is below the quarter tank mark. When I ask my daughter, she says, "I planned to get gas last night on my way home, but by the time I left the church, all stations had closed between our house and the church." If she wasn't fully honest with the goal of staying out of trouble, then it's an excuse. But if it had genuinely happened, then it's an explanation. The outcome may be the same. But the issue at hand is the motives behind the action. Who is the driver behind the response? Is she offering excuses for self-preservation or simply giving explanations for clarity?

---

[8] Jenise Harmon, "Excuse or Explanation: Is There a Difference?" *Psych Central*, 30 Aug. 2013, https://psychcentral.com/blog/your-life/2013/08/excuse-or-explanation-is-there-a-difference#1.

EXCUSES	EXPLANATIONS
Deny responsibility	Acknowledge responsibility
Seek self-preservation through defensive reasoning	Seek to explore and understand facts
Are emotion-driven	Are fact-driven

My hope is that we all pay attention. It is human nature to react based on the condition of our hearts. Everyone makes excuses at some point in life—it is part of human nature. Why do we make excuses? Excuses shift the focus from personal responsibility to a cause beyond our control. People make excuses because it's a painless way to escape a compromising situation. There is a psychology behind our excuses. If we are going to cross the bridge from "knowing" to "doing," we have to understand and overcome the emotion behind those excuses.

Excuses can be primarily traced back to one emotion: FEAR.

It's human nature to protect ourselves from the things we fear. Whether those fears are rational or irrational, our response will be the same: PROTECT! We will dive deeper into the emotion of fear a little later. For now, it's essential to know that the number one way to break our habit of making excuses is to take responsibility. Tony Robbins, a global entrepreneur and best-selling author, says it this way:

> Take responsibility. The first step to stop making excuses is always to realize that you alone control your destiny. . . . The past does not equal the future unless you live there. . . . No matter what has happened to you in the past, your future is up to you.[9]

I am thankful for the opportunity to change and go from making excuses to explanations. In my years of counseling, I have learned

---

9 Tony Robbins, "How to stop making excuses," *tonyrobbins.com*, 11 May 2021, https://www.tonyrobbins.com/productivity-performance/how-to-stop-making-excuses/.

that honesty is the first step towards change. It is okay to honestly acknowledge your heart's current condition and even explain how it got that way. You cannot allow excuses and fear to hold you back from heart health and a life of more. I can't think of a better way to set yourself up to succeed than to take an honest look at where you started, stare fear in the face, and make a conscious choice to walk away from fear and into faith. That is what it looks like to live a life of purpose.

CRUSH EXCUSES

I've taken the challenge myself. I want to crush excuses to live out God's purpose for my life in freedom. I challenge you to live a life aware of the pitfall of excuses. Crush fear, so your heart can live free. It is a place you must live every day. That is what *Guarded* is all about for me: taking another step towards the spiritual discipline and act of worship of crushing excuses. My prayer for you is that you see becoming the person God desires you to be as your responsibility.

Your heart is your responsibility! Your life tomorrow depends on the responsibility you take today! God has big plans for you tomorrow. So, make the hard choice today. Own and address everything you discover. You were created for a fantastic purpose. You are called to live your life in a way that will give God glory. Your past, present, and future are a part of that. Shame and fear are dismantled when you stop hiding behind excuses and step into more. There is a quote from Marianne Williamson's book *A Return to Love* that has stuck with me through so many seasons of life:

> Our deepest fear is not that we are inadequate. Our deepest fear is that we are powerful beyond measure. It is our light, not our darkness, that most frightens us. We ask ourselves, "Who am I to be brilliant, gorgeous, talented, fabulous?" Actually, who are you not to be? You are a child of God.

Your playing small does not serve the world. There is nothing enlightened about shrinking so that other people won't feel insecure around you. We are all meant to shine, as children do. We were born to make manifest the glory of God that is within us. It's not just in some of us; it's in everyone. And as we let our own light shine, we unconsciously give other people permission to do the same. As we are liberated from our own fear, our presence automatically liberates others.[10]

This statement reminds me to push past all my excuses and be the best me every day. God is honored when we take full responsibility for the life He has entrusted to us—a life fueled by our hearts.

PRAYER OF COMMITMENT

Heavenly Father, I choose today to take responsibility for my heart. Thank You for redeeming me from a life of sin. I surrender my heart to You. Take my history; I surrender everything to You. Help me identify the ways that my thoughts, feelings, and actions have impacted me. Give me the grace to change the areas that need to change. I release the need to make excuses. I am ready to make a change. Give me grace as I identify and surrender my heart to You in every way. In Jesus's name, I pray, AMEN.

---

10 Marianne Williamson, A Return to Love: Reflections on the Principles of "A Course in Miracles" (San Francisco, CA: HarperOne, 1996).

ECHO

*"A good man brings good things out of the
good stored up in his heart."*
—LUKE 6:45

Growing up in the summertime in a pastor's home was always memorable. We always saw family on our vacations. It was an unwritten family rule. Youth camp, church conferences, and family reunions were my summer plans. The lineup might look undesirable to you, but I loved all of it. The annual Wilson Family Reunion was at the top of my list of favorite trips. We spent a few days at Cumberland Falls State Park in Kentucky. Having dozens of family members together meant our time was full of laughter, great food, card games, and hiking in Cumberland Falls. The memories from this place are etched in my mind. Together with my sister and a couple of cousins, we covered miles of hiking trails each summer. I experienced nature, mesmerized by the wide open spaces. The beauty was never in short supply. I was always amazed by the shadows the trees cast as the sun peaked through to the forest floor. Life felt simple during those days at the Falls.

My greatest "find" at Cumberland was the falls themselves. There are dozens of walking trails all around the state park. My favorite trail took us from our cabins to the waterfalls. At one point during the 1.5-mile hike, a long run of rocks forms a cavern. It is the only place on earth I've experienced acoustics like this. The echo among those caverns was clear and concise. The caverns run directly up next to the falls. There was a walk-out platform at the end of the path. A specific spot for standing was marked for the best experience. In that place, the echo sounded like an amplified speaker system. When all factors lined up right, the echo in that place was majestic.

The quality of a sound is dependent upon the author or source of that sound. The stronger the source, the stronger the sound. The stronger the sound, the stronger the echo. Many sounds come together in this spot on the trail to make the echo stronger. The sound passed through the objects around it, the cavern, and the waterfall. Travelers from near and far would stand in that place to personally experience the sound. The echo became a symphony of sound waves, and its unique sound had to be experienced. If you ever get the opportunity to go, you should. Please go during one of the specified evenings, and you can also see the famous Moonbow Falls. They are an extraordinary sight to see as well.

I discovered several factors that made this echo unique:

1) The origin of the sound (source)
2) The quality of projected sound (sound)
3) The sounds that blend to form one unified sound (symphony)

Like the falls, our lives, spiritually and emotionally speaking, are simply the echo of our hearts! **Our lives are telling on our hearts!** Our hearts, minds, will, and emotions power our lives. They share our secrets, so no matter how hard we try to hide the innermost secrets of our hearts, they can't be hidden! Perhaps you have yet to think this through! There is always a source to every situation. A root to every problem. A stimulus that triggers every reaction. A catalyst to everything created, like the nucleus of a cell. Here's what I am getting at:

your heart is where the sound of your life comes from. The quality of the sound is determined by what is in the source. All the sounds of your heart blend to create a symphony. Did you know your life has background music?

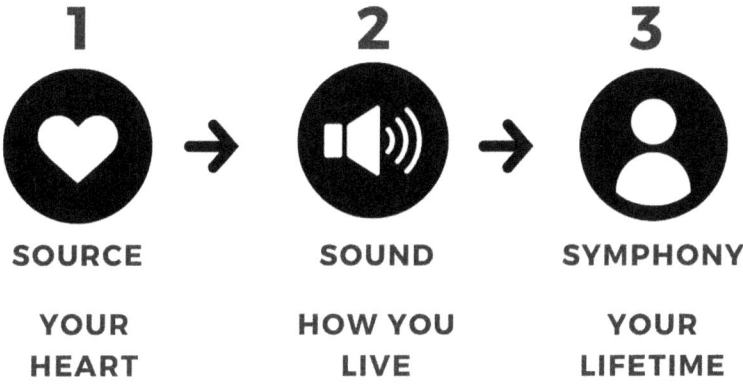

echo cycle
YOUR LIFE IS TELLING ON YOUR HEART

1 → 2 → 3
SOURCE — SOUND — SYMPHONY
YOUR HEART — HOW YOU LIVE — YOUR LIFETIME

SOURCE

Your heart is the fountain of your entire life. Proverbs 4:23 tells us our heart is the source of our life. A source is the place where everything begins. A point of origin, like the starting point of a road trip. If we are going to address the echo, we have to begin at the source.

Your heart is the source.

As pastors, we have had to mediate disagreements within the church at times. It comes with the territory of loving people. Nothing is worse than trying to work through a problem when the parties responsible are not in the room. In any meeting, if a person tries to speak for someone who isn't present, we always say, "We won't discuss that without having that person present." Things can be misrepresented when information comes through a third party. However, you can cut all the side conversations when the source is present, and a more reliable account can be provided. Sometimes, in those conversations, it takes us time to truly discover who or what the source is, but that is not the case when we live in wisdom and godly character. The Bible cuts out all the guessing and wondering. It just tells us what is. Your heart is the source.

Most of the time, the source of something lies beneath what can be seen. The engine powers the car. The engine is kept under the hood. The plumbing in your house provides the inflow and outflow of water. Plumbing is hidden behind the walls and beneath the floor. What runs your phone and computer is located inside the device. In the same way, your heart is the starting point of your life, the source of your life, and the carrier of your values; its condition must be maintained. If the source is healthy, then what is produced from it will be healthy. Likewise, if the source is unhealthy, what comes from it is unhealthy.

Several years ago, while my husband and I were cleaning the garage, water began dripping from the ceiling. The thing about water is it will always find a place to flow until it puddles, and that puddle causes a leak. It was leaking in the garage, but the problem spot was in the shower, thirty feet away from the leak. We had to remove the ceiling along the path to expose the pipes and find where the leak began. It wouldn't have been enough to fix the spot where the leak came through. We had to take the time and expense to investigate.

We had to find the source of the leak. When we did, we had to fix it. Sure, we could have left the leak at the source. But the problems would have continued. In fact, the problems would have multiplied and become so much more than a small leak.

It wasn't easy or cheap to fix, but it's our home. We are building a life here. We plan to stay and finish raising our children. We didn't give up and sell our house because of a leak. We repaired it. It was inconvenient. The renovations came at the busiest time of a pastor's life—Easter season! Due to the complexity of the leak, we had to seek outside help. Hiring a professional plumber and contractor was nonnegotiable. We quickly learned that this was not a problem we could Band-Aid.

In life, those leaks stem from our hearts. They are worth our time, effort, and attention because we build our lives on it. With our hearts, we will raise children, advance in our careers, and steward relationships. Only with our hearts can we make lasting, eternal deposits in the lives of others and accomplish God's will for our lives. Understanding the crucial role our heart plays is the starting point. Before we can continue growing it or fix the issues that lie within it, we have to understand the importance of our hearts. There are a few areas that require our attention.

Before we investigate, we have to be honest. Hopefully, you have already committed your life to Jesus. Without that, the rest will be impossible to accomplish. With Christ as your guide, you will navigate this step with assurance! His heart has restored the source of your soul. Your job is to unlearn things that weaken your heart. Open yourself up to learn how to keep your heart strong. Take your time examining your heart. Invest the resources into cultivating a healthy heart. Be intentional in focusing on true healing rather than temporary fixes. Temporary fixes give temporary relief. I want us to look at some truths about our hearts together. The source sets the standard. The source bears the standard. And the source releases/communicates the standard.

SETTING THE STANDARD

I knew my parents' expectations growing up in my home. They had boundaries and rules that they communicated regularly. I never had to question where my parents stood on an issue. They set the standard in our home. They lived it, taught it, and rewarded it when it was honored. One of my dad's many statements still rings in my ears: "Don't forget who you are, and don't forget whose you are. You were born a Martin, you are my daughter, and you are a daughter of the King; act accordingly. God loves you more than I ever could. Don't ever forget it." Growing up with stability, I didn't realize the importance of having a firm foundation. The day that became real was when I moved out on my own. I started making all my life decisions with a standard graciously given to me, but it had to become my own. (Don't get me wrong, I had standards as a child and teenager.) It was easier to live out a standard when I had people to lean on and hide behind.

> *If I am taught something, I have the head knowledge. When I experience something, it becomes heart knowledge.*

To set a standard, you have to know what you believe. Do you know what you believe? I am not talking about what you were taught to think. Do you know what YOU believe? Being taught to depend on the Lord is one thing. Having to depend on the strength of the Lord for yourself is another. If I am taught something, I have the head knowledge. When I experience something, it becomes heart knowledge. Experience turns knowledge into personal insight. It turns lessons I am taught into lessons I teach others. Heart knowledge gives me an understanding that head knowledge can't. For example, a young couple engaged to be married has an idea of marriage. The couple's understanding of marriage changes once they have experienced marriage. Gaining heart knowledge leaves a permanent mark on your heart. The imprint of heart knowledge has created a standard for the core of who I am. That standard is what will influence my desires, thoughts, feelings, and actions. Setting a standard is foundational.

Another way to look at standards is that they are boundaries that define the borders of our lives. If we are to guard our hearts, we must know the standard we guard. If I ask you to build a fence for my backyard, you must have some measurements as a starting place. You'd need to know things like how big the yard is. What is the desired material? How high will the fence be? What is the budget for the project? Without these crucial standards, who knows what could happen? I would be afraid to see the finished product—if it even could be a finished product. No one can set the boundaries for my property line but me. At the end of the day, if mismeasured, I am the only one held accountable.

So many people are going through life without setting standards. They have not decided on the boundaries they have in their life. This is causing an epidemic of heart problems. We need to set a standard to know if the inflow and outflow of our lives is healthy. Lack of clarity stiffens progress. You need to know the boundaries before you build your fence. In the same way, there is no way to walk intentionally towards growth in your life if you have no clear understanding of your boundaries.

We have told our children since they were young, "You have to decide in advance who you will be." That decision must be made intentionally in advance. When you do that, you set the standard of your life. Then, you will know how you will respond to any situation. Your standards will constantly measure your responses. When you set standards, you never have to question the decisions you make. If you do not define your standards intentionally, you give them a place to decide for you unintentionally. Your life will be all over the place. Here are some practical ways to evaluate and set your standards:

ASK YOURSELF

> Do I know what I believe? Have my beliefs come from heart knowledge or head knowledge? (What I've been taught vs. truth I've experienced).
> What knowledge has become insight gained?
> What are the standards in my life?
> Do my standards line up with God's standards?
> What standards need to change? (Added, deleted, or more closely guarded)

Our hearts can find security and safety within boundaries. Those standards protect us; they guard the gate! They give our lives the measuring stick for everything that flows in or out of it. Standards, even if unspoken, will always be seen. I am the only one who can set the standard of my heart and hold myself accountable to the boundaries I have established for it. My heart is the source, and the source sets the standard.

BEARING THE STANDARD

In the Olympic games, every country represented has a flag bearer. That person is responsible for carrying their country's emblem and flag. That individual is trusted to represent the entire Olympic team competing from that country. They will be the face that leads the way. The term "standard bearer" means one who bears a standard and leads an organization, party, or body.[11] If you describe someone as the standard bearer of a group, that means they are the leader. The one who people will look to for guidance in the group. A standard bearer sets the outsider's perception of a whole group based on their actions. In other words, they carry the standard to the world around them.

The standard bearer is the picture of our hearts because our hearts bear the standards for our spirits. They carry the standards of our lives and display them to the world around us. Our lives are not separate from the standards that we bear. The heart bears the standard, so it must be permanently marked and committed to the standard it bears. The world forms an opinion about the entire person based on the standard bearer: the heart. Luke 6:45 (NLT) tells us this: "A good person produces good things from the treasury of a good heart, and an evil person produces evil things from the treasury of an evil heart."

---

11 Merriam-Webster Dictionary Online, s.v. "standard-bearer," accessed March 11, 2024, https://www.merriam-webster.com/dictionary/standard-bearer.

It is the heart that represents the entire person. The standards we believe will be the standards we bear.

In ancient times, a king would give their signet ring to their armor bearer. When the king wanted something carried out, he would send an armor bearer. Having that signet ring was the unique mark indicating the king's approval of the person who wore it. Although the bearer used the ring, others saw only the king in the mark the signet ring would leave. The emblem on that ring was created with a family and personal insignia that announced to everyone the king's approval. The insignia changed only when the person changed, but until then, it was the appointed armor bearer who set the standard in communicating the king's approval through the mark left by the signet ring.

In the same way, our hearts bear the standards that are woven into the tapestry of our lives. Like the theme of a story, they become the theme of our lives. Our hearts become tattooed with the standard we have set for them. Those standards leave their mark on every decision, every relationship, every conversation, and every interaction a person has with us. We carry the mark of the standards we set by our authority.

 **ASK YOURSELF**

> What permanent standard is woven through the story of my life?
> In what ways do I show the standards I have set?
> Does my heart bear the permanent markings of the King (Jesus)?

COMMUNICATING THE STANDARD

To set a standard and bear a standard, we must undergo an internal change in our hearts. Communicating our standards is how we turn our hearts inside out so the world can see. I liken it to a couple in love. When a couple is dating or engaged to be married, they have not yet made a public pronouncement of a permanent union, and they won't until their wedding day. Their wedding tells the world what has transpired in their hearts. At a wedding, the guests inherently understand that the celebrated couple has dated, fallen in love, and gotten engaged. The wedding is the by-product of those commitments. The wedding communicates to the world permanence past dating and falling in love. So, the action is the communication.

In the same way, we do not have to explain our hearts to the world. Our actions, choices, and behaviors do that for us. I have never put more weight on words over actions. Don't get me wrong, sometimes words are great to hear. Words can become action if spoken intentionally and at the right time. But I have discovered that saying the right thing is easy. Backing those words up with action only happens when the source of those words is genuine. If you have been on social media for any length of time, you have seen people say many things, but words are just words. What matters are the actions that come next.

WORDS + ACTION = HEART COMMUNICATION

My husband and I pastor The Avenue Church. The Avenue is better than Disney World, to me! The people here are the best people I have ever known. I've watched God change countless lives and continue to see the ripple effect of those changes. What God is doing here reminds me of when the Queen of Sheba visited Solomon in 1 Kings 10. The Bible says that the queen witnessed something at a level that took her breath away. She was in awe of the Solomon's wisdom, the nation's prosperity, and the joy of the people. She was overwhelmed in such gratitude by King Solomon's actions that she praised God for His goodness in the king and in the people of Israel. What a challenge for believers everywhere. If the standards your heart bears were to translate into action, would those actions be awe-inspiring to others? Our mission as a church is to: show the world who Jesus is and invite them to experience His love and hope. Our mission is more than just a statement; it requires action. Anyone can make a statement. Action follows conviction and belief in the words we speak. Everything becomes apparent when you understand how to communicate your heart in this way. Both action and inaction communicate your heart.

We always tell our pastoral staff, "Don't tell people you care; show them." "Don't tell us you believe in what God has called you to do; show us." "Don't tell us you want to be trusted with more; show us." "Don't tell God you will obey no matter the cost; show Him." In our actions and inaction, we show our heart to God, family, bosses, friends, and the world around us. The sooner we all understand this small piece of life, the better off we will all be.

Many years ago, we faced a situation with a couple of leaders. When you pastor people, your love for them can become a weakness because you want them to do the right thing. It's odd how God set up spiritual authority in the church—pastoring feels strangely like parenting teenagers (except, I can't ground them from using the car, lol). The situation we faced with this couple dragged on; the leaders expressed one thing with their words, but we didn't see their actions follow suit. Of the two of us, my husband is way more tolerant of situations that require waiting. He leads with such encouragement, patience, compassion, and understanding. He leans into me to offer counsel on discernment and making wise decisions. I am thankful for our differences; we need each other to be the complete picture of Christ's love. I remember being in prayer one morning for this situation. Usually, my prayers sound like, *God, help me step back and see what I cannot see; give me the wisdom to handle people in a way that pleases You. Their words communicate one thing, but there hasn't been any action. Expose their heart and mine. This is Your church, and these are Your kids—HELP US.* If you think this is an odd prayer, you've probably never been responsible for many people or felt utterly unqualified for what God has called you to do.

> *The source sets the standard, bears the standard, and communicates the standard in your life.*

After that prayer, the Holy Spirit responded, *You already know the answer. It's right in front of you.* I remember thinking, *What did I miss?* And then it hit me: THE INACTION WAS ACTION. Through their inaction, their hearts were exposed. Their inaction was the answer. Once I feel that the Lord has settled a matter, in my mind, it's done, no matter what it looks like. Justin and I got on the same page about the situation and scheduled one last meeting. After we dealt with the situation from that point of view, the issue was completely resolved. Once the people shifted, we saw God bless the ministry and the next leaders entirely. Leading was easier.

When it was over, I had more insight than I had ever had up to that point. We can want something more for people than they want it for themselves. We can push, encourage, tolerate, be patient, and gather. If the action comes from our hearts and not theirs, we waste our time. If action isn't personal, it will never be sustainable. In other words, who I am in my heart is how I will behave. This principle is true 100 percent of the time, leaving room for mistakes and repentance. That truth doesn't stop me from wanting people to want more for their lives. But it does prevent me from trying to make my heart beat through them. Our actions, or lack thereof, communicate the standard our heart possesses.

 **ASK YOURSELF**

> What message is my heart communicating to the world?
> What are my current actions saying about the actual standards in my heart?
> What are my inactions saying about the actual standards in my heart?
> Do the standards I claim to have line up with my actions?

SOUND

All sound has a source. Sound is the result of the source releasing what it holds. The strength of the released sound depends on the health of the source. There is no other option. Sound has power and shapes the atmosphere of our lives. The loudest natural sound in the world is a volcano eruption. The raw power of an erupting volcano is awe-inspiring. Volcanos are nature's behemoths; they produce the loudest natural sounds on our planet due to the pressure from within. *BBC Science Magazine* says this about the loudest sound ever recorded:

> When the volcano Krakatoa erupted in 1883, it destroyed an island, threw debris 17 miles into the air, at a speed of half a mile a second, and killed 36,000 people. The noise it made was so loud that sailors 40 miles away suffered burst eardrums. Even 100 miles away, the volume was 170 decibels—loud enough to do lasting damage to those that heard it. And it could still be heard 3,000 miles away—the equivalent of a sound made in Britain being audible in the US.
>
> Once you get to a certain level (194 decibels, to be precise), there comes a point where the low-pressure regions are completely empty—there are no molecules in there at all. The sound can't get "louder" than *that*, technically. If there is more energy in the noise source, the air molecules are just pushed along wholesale, rather than moving back and forth, and the soundwave has turned into a shockwave. The shockwave from Krakatoa was so strong it circled the Earth four times."[12]

YOU CANNOT HIDE WHAT'S INSIDE—WHAT IS IN YOU WILL ALWAYS COME OUT

In 2003, with one semester left of college, I married my best friend. I would have told you then the same thing I would tell you today. Aside from following Jesus, marrying Justin was the best decision I've ever made. In our early days of marriage, we didn't have a lot of material possessions. What we did have was love and laughter all the time.

---

[12] What's the Loudest a Sound Can Be?," BBC Science Focus Magazine, 18 Dec. 2020, https://www.sciencefocus.com/science/whats-the-loudest-a-sound-can-be.

The apartment we lived in was built on the second story of an older home. It was a sight to behold. The layout was rather interesting. When you entered the door, you were in the living room. Immediately to the left was the door that led into the kitchen, and in the kitchen was the door to the bathroom and the washer and dryer. You could stand on one side of the living room and be six inches taller than the person on the other side. (There were no stairs in between to account for the difference.)

Justin would wake up early in the morning and get on the road to his internship, forty-five minutes away, before 6:00 a.m. I got to work at 7:00 a.m. So, I would get up, pack his lunch for him, and lay out breakfast. Once he left, I would get ready and go to work or class. I will never forget the first time I cooked dinner to surprise him. I assure you; he won't forget it either.

I come from a long line of great cooks. My great-grandmothers, grandmothers, and mom were all creative in the kitchen. Growing up, I always watched them but rarely got involved. I never had a desire to cook. I would much rather be outside working, painting, or mowing with my dad. So, not only did I lack desire, but I also needed more experience (a true recipe for disaster). How hard could it be? I had plenty of family recipes to follow. I remember this particular day as if it were yesterday. When Justin arrived home that evening, I wanted to surprise him with a homemade Mexican meal. After finishing my classes, I pulled out all the recipes I needed, made a list, and went to the store. I was excited to make an entire meal myself. Once home, I got to work slicing, dicing, mixing, and baking. The aroma filled the apartment just as he stepped through the door! *I did it!* I thought to myself. I was proud. I could tell he was proud, too. I know he was excited; food is his love language. The table was set, and the drinks were poured. All that was left was to pull the food out of the oven and put it on the table.

Opening the oven, I thought, *This smells a little stronger than I remember.* The pan of enchiladas looked and smelled great. Once I removed them and placed them on the table, I turned around to grab the Mexican corn. I had talked so much about how good this dish would be for days leading up to it. Mexican corn was a staple at most of our family gatherings. When I turned, my eyes began to water, and my nose became tingly. *Wow, this called for spice, but it has never smelled this powerful before,* I thought. *My nose may be more sensitive now.* Justin wasn't saying anything, so I assumed it was okay. We filled our plates and prayed over the meal. Until now, I had never understood why my grandmothers and great-grandmothers would cook and want to watch you eat, but all I could do was watch and wait for him to react. I am not sure what I expected, but it wasn't the reaction that happened.

> *You cannot hide what's inside.*

....

Justin took a big bite of the Mexican corn. He immediately started sniffing, his eyes began to water, and he said, "Wow, this is hot!" He tried to hide his complete shock to reassure me it was good. It was clear; he had just one bite, and his mouth was on fire. He drank a full glass of water as fast as he could. His gestures of smiling and nodding became sheer panic. Being newlyweds who were already best friends was a plus at that moment. I already knew what He was thinking. We both laughed, knowing the problem wasn't sensitivity to spice. In my trying to figure out what went wrong, I called my grandmother to verify that I had used the right ingredients. That's when it dawned on me that the recipe called for one chopped jalapeño—I used ONE WHOLE JAR. This created a big problem for the success of the dish. While baking, it looked like the meal was going to be good. When it came time to eat, the product was not as it appeared. It was ruined. All the time, ingredients, and food wasted. We had to throw the entire dish in the garbage.

I learned a few very important lessons that day. First, I had a lot to learn about cooking if I wanted to measure up to the women who had gone before me. Second, my husband is a champ. He still let me cook for him after that. Third, you cannot hide what's inside. The cooking analogy is a funny way to illustrate that what is in your heart will come out of you. You can wish it to improve, desire it to improve, and even talk about how to improve it. Recooking the corn with the right ingredients would have been the only way to make it amazing. This is also true of our lives.

What is going on around a person is going on inside a person. Another way to say that is that situations happening around a person are happening within them first. What is coming from us changes the landscape around us. Of course, there are always exceptions to every rule of thumb, but it is true—99 percent of the time if something is always happening around you, it is happening within you. How does this happen? Through our actions and our words. Remember: thoughts, feelings, and actions—the brain reasons these three components through the lens of your heart.

Your heart is playing a theme song. The melody plays through the choices you make, the relationships you choose, the places you go, the words you speak, the habits you form, the goals you set, the results you achieve, and the spirit you possess. The melody of your heart will change the atmosphere of your entire life. Reading this either brought a smile to your face or silence. If you are smiling, turn up the song and dance.

Are you ready for the great news? If you don't like the song, you can change the station (aka the source—your heart). I would never leave you to suffer in silence. If the sound coming from your life hurts your ears, improve it, and keep pushing forward. We are in this together.

Sound = The Melody that Flows from My Heart and Creates the Echo

ASK YOURSELF

› What is the theme song flowing from your heart based on your present life?
› Evaluate the areas above, circle any areas in your life where you know the melody needs to change.

SYMPHONY

I love music. I've always enjoyed a variety of genres. My mom's side of the family has incredible musical ability. My nana has found a way to get a song going at every gathering since I was a child. Once the song was identified, everyone eventually joined in with a different part. The fun part was that everyone sang a different part, and when the sounds came together, it was a beautiful symphony of voices. Music was a part of our gatherings because musical talent ran through our DNA. It was inside of us. It became a symphony because all the parts came together. One voice was only a part, but everyone together created an unbelievable sound.

Much like a symphony, our lives are full of many sounds that create a masterpiece. Most of the sounds have come from our hearts. Some situations you and I have faced have been out of our control. We sometimes have to deal with the result of someone else's choice. However, others' choices do not have to create the sheet music for the orchestra. Even our own failures don't have to ruin our story, just like a few sour notes don't have to ruin a song. What determines the greatness of the song is how the orchestra recovers after a wrong note is played. Practice. Learn. Grow. Keep releasing the sound. The next note will be better.

The longer we live, the more opportunity we have to create a song that tops the charts. You are not your worst note. You can't shut it down and quit. It would be best if you yielded to the conductor, our heavenly Father. A musician only quits when they focus on themselves. Focus on the conductor and follow His lead. Get your eyes on Him, cry, get frustrated and angry, and then get better. Learn what tripped you up and improve. Our worst moments do not have to defeat our lives; what we do after our worst moments defines them. Great things can come from failures.

I came across a fun article that listed a couple dozen songs that were failures or written on accident, but they still topped the charts:

> The intro for Guns N' Roses' "Sweet Child of Mine" has become one of the most recognizable guitar riffs of all time. While many people think it came from a stroke of genius from guitarist Slash, he claims the opposite. He admitted that the opening riff was just a string-skipping exercise he was practicing during a casual jam session.
>
> When Axl Rose heard it, he came running in saying he already had lyrics and that it would be their next hit. The

song didn't take them long to finish, especially since the last half is Rose repeating the lyrics "where do we go now?" The song peaked at No. 1 and made their debut album the top-selling album of all time.[13]

The Bible is full of great examples of recovering from failure! The entire family line of our Savior was full of mistakes, failures, and sins until Jesus came. That gives me HOPE! Jesus changes everything. The role of the conductor in a symphony is also referred to as the maestro, which is Italian for "master." Our value was already determined when the Master chose us. He died so we could rise from our failures. He stands on the platform of our lives, ready to lead us to the performance for which we were created. He holds our next move. His baton is in hand, ready to direct each story's tempo, volume, and dynamic. We get to choose if we will follow. He knows you. He knows the source of your sound and is ready to bring all the sounds of your life together in a beautiful musical arrangement!

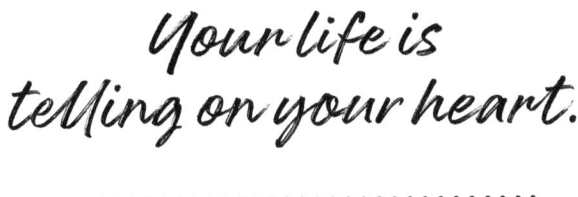

Your life is telling on your heart.

Symphony = The Life Created When All Sounds Merge

---

13 Happy Accidents That Made Songs and Musicians into Major Hits,'" *purevolume*, accessed March 4, 2024 https://www.purevolume.com/music/happy-accidents-that-made-songs-and-musicians-into-major-hits/.

 **ASK YOURSELF**

> What are some of the "bad notes" in life that I need to surrender to be used by the Master?
> Do you trust Master to direct you through the entire arrangement?

The source, the sound, and the symphony determine the echo of our lives. Your life is telling on your heart. We need these areas to be strong, positive, and balanced. Then, our lives become a reflection of our Creator. We can show Jesus to the world through our lives.

HEALTH CHECK

Doctors must run multiple medical tests for a person who has heart issues. The tests aim to get a clear picture of what is happening inside. The safest, most reliable test is an echocardiogram (echo). An echo is an ultrasound test that checks the structure and function of your heart. It can diagnose a range of conditions and diseases. Cleveland Clinic says:

> *An echocardiogram (echo) is a graphic outline of your heart's movement. During an echo test, your healthcare provider uses ultrasound (high-frequency sound waves) from a hand-held wand placed on your chest to take pictures of your heart's valves and chambers. The echo helps the provider evaluate the pumping action of your heart. Providers often combine echo with Doppler ultrasound and*

color Doppler techniques to evaluate blood flow across your heart's valves.[14]

A doctor could order an echo for any reason:
- You have symptoms of heart disease.
- You have been diagnosed with a problem in need of further examination.
- A clear picture of all angles of your heart is needed.
- Your heart strength needs checking before you undergo a surgical procedure.

The medical world is fascinating. An echocardiogram can catch and diagnose any form of heart disease, valve disease, heart defect, blood clot, or aneurysm. Doctors can diagnose all of that from an echo! The direction of sound waves might change in an echo, but it will send back a blueprint of the heart. Imagine how many heart attacks and deaths the echo test has prevented. What excellent news for us!

We can allow our heavenly Father to perform an echo on our hearts. He can go straight to the source! Christ can go past all the issues and behaviors and show us the source of the problem. Our heart is what He is after because He sees past everything in our lives straight to the source. First Samuel 16 takes us to a time when the Lord talks to Samuel about picking a king to replace Saul. When Samuel begins, God addresses his humanness. Samuel calls the sons of Jesse, who look like kings. But God tells Samuel, "I don't see things like you see them. I see in ways much more profound than you. You can't see what I see, and that is why you need Me." What a powerful reminder that what lies beneath the surface is what God sees first. God bases His judgment of our lives on our hearts. God's approval or disapproval of humanity is based on the source, not the

---

[14] Cleveland Clinic medical professional, "Echocardiogram: Types and What They Show," *Cleveland Clinic*, accessed April 12, 2024, https://my.clevelandclinic.org/health/diagnostics/16947-echocardiogram.

side effects. A heart check is needed regularly. The best time to check the echo is NOW.

PRAYER OF COMMITMENT

Heavenly Father, thank You for the wisdom found in Your Word. It is my desire that my heart be an echo of Your goodness to the world. May the standards of my life be pleasing to You. Show me where the sound coming from my heart needs to improve. I want the symphony of my life to be a masterpiece. Look in my heart, show me areas where issues hide, and give me the boldness to address them. I give You control. My life is Yours in Jesus's name, AMEN.

HEART INVADERS

"If our hearts condemn us, we know that God is greater than our hearts, and He knows everything."
—1 JOHN 3:20

We all have issues (and sometimes, we must evaluate what we have let into our hearts to cause those issues). If we don't do regular heart checks, it is only a matter of time before problems will surface. When those problems happen, remember that what is in us will come from us. Let's pick up our discussion on the echocardiogram and go one step further.

The doctor who performs the echo is called a sonographer. Through the device in the sonographer's hand, sound waves are sent to the heart. The sound waves bounce back, revealing a clear picture of what the eye cannot see. The picture lets the sonographer know precisely where the issues are located. When the location is known, the issue can be addressed. The diagnosis gives us a starting point for healing and a roadmap for health. The picture of our life today is simply an echo of our hearts! We will pay attention to our hearts if we desire a healthy life. The time to fix the issue is now. We don't want to wait for a catastrophe to happen.

Today, we can become spiritual and emotional sonographers. We will look at some invaders that attack our hearts. They come with intentions to destroy and steal our lives. My prayer is that you will see the authority and power available to you to destroy these invaders. We must search for the invaders in our hearts, identify them, and eliminate them. If we are committed to the process, we can receive total healing and freedom.

INVADER ALERT

Invader: Someone or something who enters by force in order to conquer. An intruder or trespasser.

Growing up in a pastor's home had its ups and downs. There are negatives and positives in every life. Ninety-nine percent of the time, I loved being a pastor's kid. (It meant we got to go through the food line first on Pastor Appreciation Day!) My parents pastored a church in a small town in Tennessee, and we lived in a church parsonage. In case you are not aware, a parsonage is a house on church property given to a pastor's family to live in. A church parsonage is a 24/7 emergency clinic, counseling office, and benevolence center; at least, that is what some members of the congregation believe. As a child, I remember people dropping by unannounced. Sometimes, the drop-ins brought us fresh produce or food. Others stopped by for assistance in their emergency or crisis. No matter the reason, I always felt the same feeling—a total invasion of my privacy.

Home has always been my safe space. There is no better feeling after a long day than going home. Home is where you can take off every title and expectation from the world around you and just rest. As a pastor's kid, you must share your parents with the church and its members. At that time, home meant something extra special: a place to have mom and dad all to ourselves. Each time anyone showed up at my home unannounced, I was anxious. Their arrival felt like a complete invasion of our personal space. For the most part, people meant well. But you never knew if the next invader would walk in and whisk your parents away to help them. An all-night counseling session with their fighting relatives. Prayer for an injury that needed stitches. Help with grocery money or finances to fix their car. Advice about what to do in a particular situation. Or, just a good citizen offering a stray dog he found on the road. (I think you get the picture.) No matter how big or small the issue, all of them were invasions of my personal safe space. They were intrusions on sacred ground. It's not that their concerns were insignificant, though some of them were. It was how they forced themselves into our space. Maybe no one had ever taught them consideration or to think of others. Perhaps they knew better and just didn't do better. It's possible people thought the church paid us to be at their disposal. Whatever their reason, the intruders came.

In the name of doing "good" or "caring for others," we often lose all guardrails. I am not referring to one isolated event to help someone. Our family loved people, and we still love people. In fact, my sister and I both went into full-time ministry and live our lives to love people. I have since learned that sometimes, we can allow people, mindsets, and actions to intrude on our well-being. When we don't stop an intruder, we invite them to steal. How crazy would it be if someone attempted to break into your house and you just let them in—to not be seen as unkind? No call to 911. No guns blazing. You open the door and allow them to steal whatever they'd like. Partnering with an intruder would be crazy, right? Of course, it would be—an intruder is not a friend!

This simple fact is true for our physical, mental, and spiritual lives. Intruders are not there to grow us. Intruders are enemies on assignment to ravage our well-being! Scripture tells us in John 10:10 that "the thief comes only to steal and kill and destroy." The enemy of your faith is not asking permission to come in; he just shows up. In a moment of weakness, he overruns the vulnerable state of your heart. He is not kind. He is not considerate. Your enemy wants only one thing: to get in. First Peter 5:8 (ESV) says, "Be sober-minded; be watchful. Your adversary the devil prowls around like a roaring lion, seeking someone to devour." I find it interesting that the enemy of our soul is described in two ways in scripture: a thief (John 10:10) and a prowling lion (1 Peter 5:8). Based on those scriptures, that tells us two things: the enemy operates in darkness, and the enemy disguises himself and hides. Understanding this exposes everything. Knowing his plan allows us to be on guard and ready for the attack.

INVADERS OPERATE IN DARKNESS

As we read in Scripture, lions prowl for their victims. They sleep twenty hours a day and hunt at night. To their advantage, their eyes are designed to see better at night. Lions are hidden and calculated. They lay in the shadows and wait for their prey. Hunting at night allows them to sneak up on their sleeping prey to catch them off guard.[15] Scripture doesn't say anything by accident. God wants us to win over our enemy and gives us the playbook to do so.

My husband is a huge college football fan. I have learned to love football as well. He always says one thing to me when a great team with a winning record loses: "Anyone can be beaten on any given day. Winning is determined by who shows up ready to play and has spent time off the field studying the other team. Winning is about learning and knowing how to outplay your opponent."

Meanwhile, the lion's prey can do nothing to change their eyesight or become nocturnal. They beat the lion in the darkness by getting ready in the light. They develop and adapt to protect themselves from

---

15 Daniel Vernick, "How loud is a lion's roar? And 4 other lion facts," *WWF*, accessed May 16, 2024, https://www.worldwildlife.org/stories/how-loud-is-a-lion-s-roar-and-4-other-lion-facts.

becoming a lion's dinner. They stick with other animals who assist with being on guard. They have developed heightened sensitivity that warns them of danger. They learn where not to go and how to camouflage with nature. Some prey even use defensive weapons or behaviors that protect them.

The enemy who prowls around like a lion doesn't have new plays. He is predictable, not wise, not all-knowing, and unconcerned about your pain or suffering—the opposite of anything resembling God's character. He wants to devour and take away pieces of you. His pleasure is your downfall. But there is good news. Because we know his strategy, we can beat him at his own game.

How can we beat him at his own game? First, your entire mind and perspective have to be VICTORY. When Christ died and rose again, He gave us the victory. He intended for us to live IN that victory. That means we should see our enemy from a place of victory. That victory is for all time. It is not conditional. His sacrifice was for all humanity until eternity. If that is the case, what keeps people from being victorious? Great question, here's the answer: it's a choice! A choice to say, "I will live in victory." A choice to read God's Word so you know the playbook. And a choice to live in obedience to the Word to turn on the light.

The second way to beat your enemy is to shine a light. Light dispels darkness. Wildlife experts will tell you that if you encounter a lion at night, you need to shine your light in its eyes, keep it there, and back away. Don't just turn and run because the lion will pursue you. This knowledge gets me so fired up. "Wait, Melissa, are you telling me it's that simple to defeat the enemy with light?" YES. I can prove it. Psalm 119:105 (ESV) says, "Your word is a lamp to my feet and a light to my path." His Word is the light. His Word has power. His Word is alive and active. Hebrews 10 tells us that. But a light is just a light until it is used for a purpose. It must become personal. It has to go from being a light to being your light.

> *When truth confronts a lie, it unravels.*

Even the devil himself knows the Word of God. He used the Word against Jesus in the wilderness when Jesus went away to fast and pray for forty days. But he can't use God's Word as a place of victory; the truth is not in him. In other words, the enemy used the Word of God to manipulate, but Jesus used the Word to annihilate. When truth confronts a lie, it unravels. Jesus showed us that by speaking the truth of Scripture back to the enemy. He turned on His light, picked up His victory, and threw it in the face of the enemy to shatter the lies and manipulation.

Christ *told us* and *showed us* how to defeat darkness. So how do we prepare for the invader to come in darkness? When 1 Peter tells us to be sober and watchful, he tells us he will come. It is not a maybe; it's a guarantee. We can get excited when we see this from a place of victory! We have already won. Our job is to pick up our light, GOD's Word, to ensure the enemy will not devour us. Let the truth of Scripture shine so bright through our lives that it blinds the enemy. And walk in that light. We have victory, we win, and winning has a way of silencing enemies. The invader of darkness is defeated when a believer lives his life in light and victory.

INVADERS CASE AND WAIT

Lions and thieves (John 10:10) study the habits and rhythms of their prey. Thieves have one goal: to steal. Depending on what they are after, creating a plan to enter your home will take time. When we moved into our home, we installed an alarm system. The ADT representative mapped where and how we wanted the sensors, cameras, and keypad. He spent an entire day installing the system and then returned on a second day to teach us how to use it. We pay ADT a monthly monitoring service to watch over our home. Here is the point: we didn't get an alarm system installed in our home to catch the thief robbing us. We have ADT to prevent our home from being robbed at all. Suppose someone intends to break into my home; they will case and wait. That means they will watch you, study your habits, and learn your routine. They do all that to break in and take the most valuable items in the home.

The enemy of your soul is the same way. He is watching and waiting. He dangles temptation as bait to learn what you like. When you bite, he pulls the line and catches you in his trap. I have heard a saying all my life: sin will take you further than you wanted to go, cost you more than you wished to pay, keep you longer than you wanted to stay and laugh at you when you get there. In other words, the enemy wants to take everything from you and kick you when you are down.

Just like we pay for an alarm system in our homes, we must have one in our lives—sensors that tell us when we have opened a door that needs to be closed. We need warning sirens that go off when our lines of defense are broken. First Corinthians 10:13 is a promise God gave us: "No temptation has overtaken you that is not common to man. God is faithful, and he will not let you be tempted beyond your ability, but with the temptation he will also provide the way of escape, that you may be able to endure it" (ESV). God has an escape room! A promised exit. A place of safety. A place we can hide when the enemy attempts to break in. Remember, the enemy isn't all-knowing. He only knows what we show and tell. We show our weakness when we fall to sin. We tell him how to trap us when that sin is habitual.

Habitual sin is a sin committed on repeat. It can be packaged differently or introduced in different ways, but we still fall prey to it. If there is any weakness in our lives and we haven't run to the escape room, eventually, we will fall. This type of lifestyle means we do the enemy's work for him. He doesn't have to try and entice us or even break in; we invite him to remain in our lives.

I have seen people carry this type of sin throughout their lives. I have seen it become generational and destroy so many lives. Habitual sin comes from seeds within our hearts. It is a thought turned into a feeling and then an action, and it becomes a cycle on repeat. According to the Bible, if a person is controlled by habitual sin, they aren't in a relationship with Christ: "No one who is born of God will continue to sin, because God's seed remains in them; they cannot go on sinning, because they have been born of God" (1 John 3:9).

I am not here to discourage you but to show that accidental and repetitive sin are very different. The only way the enemy can entice you repeatedly with the same sin is if you remain in the wrong place. God provided a way of escape. God's way equals safety, security, and life. Self-denial isn't even powerful enough to break habitual sin. Habitual sin can be broken by surrendering to Christ and fostering a genuine heart desire for something greater. In his article "The Secret to Breaking Free from Habitual Sin," John Bloom said this:

> Every sin, every wrongdoing, no matter what kind—whether acted out in behavior or nurtured secretly in some dark place of our heart (Matthew 5:28)—is a manifestation of something we believe. Every sin is born out of a belief that

disobeying God (wrongdoing) will produce a happier outcome than obeying God (right-doing). Whether or not we're conscious of this, it's true. Nobody sins out of duty.[16]

We must know our hearts and identify the places we have allowed invaders to dwell. In the darkness, we must turn on the light. If an enemy is lying in wait for an opportunity to break in, sound the alarm. Go on lockdown. We are talking about your heart, the source of your life and the keeper of eternity. Protect it! We have to have our defenses ready. Remember, we purchased our alarm system to keep thieves from ever coming our way. We are sending them the message: "This house is secure!" We must eliminate the invaders in our hearts that break down our defenses. It's time to send invaders a message: this heart is steadfast and secure. . . . it is GUARDED!

If you are brave, you will search every corner of your heart for invaders. Ask the Holy Spirit to search your heart, and then ask Him to show you what He sees. I know from experience that He will search and show you what needs to change. If a better tomorrow and a life alive with purpose entices you, you will enthusiastically obey. As followers of Christ, obedience to his Word isn't an option; it's an expectation. I can say yes to him with a willing heart, or I can say yes and pray that my mind and heart follow. Either way, the believer's answer to God's correction should always be yes.

My prayer for you, as you search, is that you would be humble to hear His voice because it's truth. Be courageous enough to challenge your beliefs and bold enough to make a change in your boundaries. When the rubber meets the road, change always depends on our actions! Actions hinge on beliefs. A successful guarding of our hearts depends on our boundaries.

---

[16] Jon Bloom, "The Secret to Breaking Free from Habitual Sin," *Desiring God*, 29 June 2019, https://www.desiringgod.org/articles/the-secret-to-breaking-free-from-habitual-sin.

BELIEF STEERS BEHAVIOR

We discussed belief briefly when we looked at thoughts, feelings, and actions. We can spend minimal time here regarding our response to the truth in God's Word. The only standards we live by are the truths we believe. When protecting our hearts from intruders, we must challenge every belief in our hearts. The best way to do that is to work backward: isolate a behavior, investigate the belief behind it, weigh it with God's Word, and respond to its truth. Remember, truth is a light, and light dispels darkness. Be brave enough to admit when your beliefs are wrong and repent. If we do, God's faithfulness cleanses us, and we get a chance to reset our boundaries around truth.

No one has a perfect life, no matter how people portray their lives in the public eye. You may have asked yourself these questions: *Is everyone dealing with this? Does anyone else feel this way? Am I the only one who _____ (fill in the blank)?* If you have asked these questions, I assure you that you are not alone. There are roughly 8.1 billion people on planet Earth.[17] No matter where we are, our age, gender, or race, we all have this in common: we are all human. God's Word confirms that we will all face trials and temptations. Believers and nonbelievers in Christ alike will endure hardships, joy, blessings, and pain. All these things are guaranteed because we are human. We were born human, and we will die human. If we have given our hearts to Christ, death in body is not the end of life with Him.

The heart of a believer must be different, under constant evaluation by the Holy Spirit. Our humanness can never win over our souls. Only our souls are eternal. Assessment of your heart and motives is imperative. This assessment happens through prayer and reflection. We can ask God the way David asked in Psalms 139:23 (ESV), "Search

---

[17] "Current World Population," *Worldometer*, accessed June 13, 2024, https://www.worldometers.info/world-population/.

me, O God, and know my heart! Try me and know my thoughts!" If we can catch a wrong belief before it takes root in our hearts, we will save ourselves a lot of pain. The deeper the roots grow, the more painful the pruning. We are living this life to prepare for eternity. While we are here circling the sun, we are responsible for the life we live. Our hearts must stay laid before our heavenly Father. We must be honest with ourselves. We must allow the Holy Spirit to change us continually. This is the mindset of pruning: if it isn't okay with You, Jesus, it's not okay with me.

BOUNDARIES

All creation has boundaries, such as the laws of nature, scientific property, physical property, human relationships, and even our emotional well-being. God set boundaries when He stepped up onto the creation platform in Genesis 1. He assigned boundaries to everything He created. Everything living had to operate in the confines of those boundaries.

If God sets the boundary, we who keep it are wise.

Until the fall of Adam and Eve, everything was perfect. And here we have again the result of sin. It changed everything. Instead of an ideal world, it was now a fallen world. The freedom of choice and knowledge of good and evil are at humanity's disposal. God's original boundaries were perfection. Adam and Eve crossed those perfect boundaries, and the world has struggled ever since. The fall should teach us that if God sets the boundary, we who keep it are wise. Keeping God's boundaries equals life. Like a good father, the boundaries He sets are for our benefit. Crossing them opens our hearts to the enemy.

Boundaries are wisdom on display. They demonstrate honor and respect for the belief inside your heart. Whether spoken or unspoken, boundaries are the lines that define what behaviors are acceptable for an individual. Boundaries can be physical (e.g., don't touch me), emotional (e.g., do not speak to me in that tone), or spiritual (e.g., I will not participate; I don't feel good about it). Boundaries should be set in every relationship and every activity. The boundaries in your life must be set and enforced from a place of personal awareness and conviction. The lack of boundaries is uncaring and detrimental to you and the world around you.

Our walk with Christ is our responsibility. Growing in understanding of His Word is an expectation if we are going to succeed. We will learn more about His character the longer we pursue and serve Him. He fills the Scriptures with instructions on how to avoid being a victim of heart invaders. Sometimes, these invaders come through invitation. And sometimes, they come in through weak defense systems. No matter how they arrive, they have one intention: to destroy. Intruders come to ravage your heart and destroy your life. Change is available for you today.

IDENTIFYING HEART INVADERS

INVADER OF FEAR

Fear comes to destroy our faith. What is fear? Fear is the unpleasant feelings you experience when you think you are in danger. It is a nagging feeling that something terrible will happen. There are several types of fear: fear of God (healthy), fear that keeps us safe (healthy), and fear that prevents growth (unhealthy). The Bible tells us that "the fear of the LORD is the beginning of wisdom" (Proverbs 9:10, NKJV). Fear of the Lord is a healthy fear. It is this fear that leads us to honor and revere His holiness. Another healthy type of fear is the fear that keeps you safe (i.e., don't touch the stove when it is hot). This fear keeps us from living careless lives. Both healthy types of fear partner with wisdom. The third type of fear is unhealthy—it prevents growth or forward motion.

This unhealthy fear keeps us from obeying, growing, and walking in faith. According to the American Heart Association, in extreme cases, it is physically possible for a person's heart to stop from fear.[18] Interestingly, the unhealthy fear I am referring to does the same. This fear comes to our spiritual and emotional lives to stop our hearts from beating. Fear's job is to paralyze us. Scripture tells us in James 2:20 (NKJV) that "faith without works is dead." The invader of fear stops our work by freezing us in our tracks. Fear paralysis is rooted in a lack of clarity in who God is in our lives. It puts the focus on us and blurs our view of Christ.

God has more for all of us. Have you ever felt God calling you deeper? It seems easy to say yes to that question until you come face to face with the true meaning of "deeper." I will always remember August 2012. Our family of four left everything we had known to respond to God's invitation to more. We had lived in Cincinnati for the previous nine years. Our kids were four and five years old. Everything in life felt like it couldn't get better, until one day, out of nowhere, everything shifted. My husband and I both felt God call us to move from Ohio to Tennessee to pastor. We were already in ministry and loved the place God had us serving in Cincinnati. There was no reason for a shift. We never saw it coming.

---

[18] "Can You Really Be Scared to Death?" *American Heart Association*, 31 Oct. 2018, https://www.heart.org/en/news/2018/10/31/can-you-really-be-scared-to-death#:~:text=Every%20year%20around%20Oct.,to%20happen%20from%20Halloween%20hijinks.

What I love about radical faith is that it's wild and unexplainable. Radical steps of faith leave no room for focus on self. Your entire line of vision has to stay on Christ. Failure to keep your eyes on Christ would be like climbing the tallest ladder and looking down to see no supports holding you up. With our eyes on Christ, we gave God our yes. Anytime faith is released and followed, fear is close by, waiting to invade—and that is precisely what happened.

I remember it like it was yesterday. Once we arrived in Tennessee, everything felt unstable. People who promised to walk beside us walked away. Suddenly, everything we believed God was working out for us felt lifeless. My husband had no employment, and I took a job that was $20,000 less than what I was making in Ohio. We looked crazy! Living in my in-laws' basement, we had no money and could not tell people what was next. I would love to tell you that our faith never wavered. That following God in faith was easy and smooth. But that wouldn't be accurate.

> *The root of fear forges deeper into our hearts when our need to control the outcome is more significant than our belief that He's in control.*

Uncertainty is difficult for human brains. There were several nights I fell asleep with tears streaming down my face. I felt fear doing all it could to get me to turn back. Thoughts like: *What have you done? You were so sure God called you! It was all in your mind. You have ruined everything. You all missed it. What will everyone think of you?* For three months, the fear never let up. There were days it felt like God had forgotten us like men had, and there were days we failed and entertained fear in our minds, but our faith in what God spoke never wavered. When I felt fear, my husband stood in faith. When he fought fear, I stood in faith. Thank God we never had a bad day at the same time. (If so, we wouldn't be in Tennessee today.) We can't take ground from the enemy living in fear. We have to look past fear into our future and let faith propel us into more. Ultimately, that is what we chose to do!

In the end, what matters is that we got back up and kept moving. Looking back, I see it all so clearly, Facing fear is not where things go wrong. What goes wrong is when fear takes root in your heart and grows so deep that it chokes out hope. In that moment, the enemy came to stop what he knew our act of faith would produce. The enemy sent the intruder of fear in our weakest moments. When we focus on ourselves, fear shows us everything we are not. But when faith kicks in, all we see is Jesus, our living Hope. Faith that isn't tested isn't alive. If you can do what God has called you to do in your strength, then it's not faith; it's obedience.

Fear will always be present when great faith is required. We must keep fear from taking root and setting camp in our hearts. If we allow fear to take root, we become paralyzed. I have learned there is a greater chance of fear becoming rooted when we have to be in control. The root of fear forges deeper into our hearts when our need to control the outcome is more significant than our belief that He's in control. Wisdom says to trust and walk in faith; His way is better. Fear says, "Wait, don't move. You can't control the outcome."

If you are going to be a person of faith, you will have to remove the intruder of fear.

1) **Investigate Your Heart** (Honesty): Are there any areas of my life where I am allowing fear to paralyze me?
2) **Challenge Your Beliefs** (Truth): John 14:27; Hebrews 11; Mark 4:35-41
3) **Set and Enforce Your Boundaries** (Wisdom): I will choose to step in faith using wisdom as my guide. I will remember that when faith is required, fear is always present to try and paralyze me. I will move in faith and give God control.

INVADER OF BUSYNESS

Busyness comes to steal our purpose. How many times have we been guilty of saying: "I'm just so busy, I don't have time for anything." If you haven't said it, you are ahead of the curve, congratulations. I've said it and heard it from so many people. We wear busyness as a badge of honor. Many times, we use busyness to build our self-esteem. Staying busy doesn't mean we are accomplishing anything of purpose. It is easy to get caught up in the busyness of life. Busyness is to be in a state of excess with much to do. Excess is a word I see everywhere I look. People are spending and working in excess to try to pay off debt. We live in a society that is raising kids in excess. "If you want it, do it," is the mantra. We excessively cram our schedules. We are running at a sprint runner's pace, forgetting that life is a marathon. We are navigating crammed schedules: work, family, sporting events, parties, work, practice, kids' ballgames, church, work, travel, vacations, work, me-time, and so on. You get the picture. None of those things are wrong, but all those things are not right, either.

> *When our wants don't align with God's, what should have the most focus will often have the least.*

Busyness is an enemy that slides in under false pretense. All the things we are doing are good! I have had people tell me their families must "do" all they are doing if they want to keep up with others. I understand that all of us face busy seasons. However, our constant state of busyness is detrimental to our hearts. Physical, mental, emotional, relational, and spiritual consequences will befall those who choose this pace of life. The physical consequences of busyness mostly come from lack of sleep, proper nutrition, and poor diet. Chronic stress is also a real issue that causes symptoms physically and emotionally, mimicking a heart attack.[19] Excessive busyness can hurt our mental health. It can cause feelings such as anxiety, hopelessness, loneliness, frustration, inadequacy, anger, and guilt.[20]

Our relationships can suffer due to the invasion of busyness. We can begin to feel isolated and disconnected. When we rush from one thing to the next, we lack quality time with our family and friends. And if all of this doesn't sound detrimental enough, let's take our spiritual lives as an example. When our wants don't align with God's, what should have the most focus will often have the least.

---

[19] "Stress symptoms: Effects on your body and behavior," *Mayo Clinic*, accessed 11 Jul 2024, https://www.mayoclinic.org/healthy-lifestyle/stress-management/in-depth/stress-symptoms/art-20050987.

[20] Jodi Clarke, "How Constantly Staying Busy Affects Our Well-Being," *Verywell Mind*, 21 Nov 2023, https://www.verywellmind.com/how-the-glorification-of-busyness-impacts-our-well-being-4175360.

From the Old Testament to Revelation, God's expectations are clear. He is supposed to be the center of our hearts and lives. Our lives are to revolve around him. We will have to "fit" Him into our schedules. His day every week is holy; we have to shift our schedules to meet that expectation. Our purpose is eternal! One day, all the busyness in our schedules will fade away, and only what is eternal will count. We will stand before Him. We will answer for how well we stewarded our lives, children, and those He trusted to our care. We will be accountable. It should make you think twice about the priorities in your life. It brings a holy fear over my heart. Have you prayed about the items that fill your calendar? Have you made giving to His Kingdom a priority? Have you raised your children with the understanding that God's expectations are to be obeyed and honored? If your children honored your expectations the way you honor God's, would they be grounded?

"He must increase, but I must decrease" (John 3:30, NKJV). My purpose can never be realized putting myself first. His purpose for my life becomes clear when He is first. We defeat the invader of busyness by living our purpose. Our priorities must begin and end with Christ. When the Pharisees asked Jesus what the greatest commandment was, His response was full of purpose. Matthew 22:37 (NKJV) says, "Jesus said to him, 'You shall love the Lord your God with all your heart, with all your soul, and with all your mind.'" We must obey His order. Him first. If He is first, life will be full of eternal purpose. Life is never going to offer you a break. If you want your life to be pleasing to Christ, you must intentionally ask. Ask Him to show you the right priorities. Ask Him to help you see where you have chosen your plans over His. If you are going to live a life of purpose, you will have to take out the intruder of busyness. Your discipline will block the intruder of busyness!

1) **Investigate Your Heart** (Honesty): Is the intruder of busyness keeping me from right priorities and purpose?
2) **Challenge Your Beliefs** (Truth): John 3:30; Matthew 6:33; Matthew 6:21; Philippians 3:8.
3) **Set and Enforce Your Boundaries** (Wisdom): I will ask the Lord to show me what my life's priorities should be. I will honor God's expectations first. I will slow down to ensure my well-being in every way. I will choose purpose.

INVADER OF UNWORTHINESS

Your value is not based on physical things you possess, by what you accomplish, or on any character trait. Your worth has been assigned to you by your Creator. You are His—loved and chosen. Your worth isn't dependent on you. The idea that we must be "good enough" to earn our worth is the opposite of the gospel. He determined our worth at creation. Jesus confirmed our worth on the cross, and He will return for us because we are the object of His affection. He wouldn't do any of that for something of low value. We must open our eyes to this truth when we believe in Christ. Truth is the only way to overcome the intruder of unworthiness. To allow negative beliefs of our worth to invade our lives is detrimental. Jesus placed a high value on our hearts. He died to redeem them. No one and nothing can change our worth.

Unworthiness comes to steal our belief in our worth. Shame accompanies it as a twin. It can attempt to invade early in life through abuse, trauma, events in childhood, wrong mindsets, or sins we've committed.[21] It comes to us disguised by shame, but the two work hand in hand. Unworthiness causes us to hide. We saw this in the garden once Adam and Eve sinned; shame caused them to hide from

---
21 Oak Health Foundation, "How to Overcome Feelings of Unworthiness," *Oak Health Foundation*, 26 Feb. 2024, https://www.oakhealthfoundation.org/how-to-overcome-feelings-of-unworthiness.

God (Genesis 3). Your value remains no matter what you have done or what has been done to you. It is that value that makes your enemy afraid. I have seen this trick of the enemy up close and personal in the lives of so many people. This invader brings shame and condemnation. Owning unworthiness and feeling like you don't measure up to who you should be will cause you to struggle with low self-esteem. When unworthiness invades your life, it causes you to settle for less than you deserve and compare yourself to others.

Have you ever met a person who you immediately knew would be significant in your life? That happened the day I met Kristen. Kristen is now on our pastoral staff team at The Avenue. She is one of the most dedicated and passionate people I know. She is called by God and walks out her calling in a beautiful way. But she wasn't always this way. She has grown so much since we met her just seven years ago. I can remember the first time she walked into our church. She was intelligent, hungry to serve, and fun, but distant. She did everything she could to hide. Try as we may, the true calling of God on our lives cannot be hidden.

As I got to see her in action, I quickly realized she had so much inside of her that she intended to hide. I knew it was time for me to know her story. What I learned made everything clear. Kristen was raised in church and called by God into ministry as a teenager. After she gave God her yes, she had allowed mistakes, sin, and shame to tell her she wasn't worthy of her calling. For ten years, she silenced the longing to see the dream of ministry come to pass. If you have ever been called to something, you know the ache and longing that never leaves your heart. It's impossible to silence.

You are not crazy, sinful, or intelligent enough to silence it. Romans 11:29 says that "God's gifts and his call are irrevocable." He again showed us that our worth doesn't come from how good we are! God alone gives us our worth and calling. Yes, we will reap the consequences of our sins. Some of us take the long road to God's destination for us, but He alone is sovereign; His ways are higher. His call and His plan are without repentance. He is not in heaven waiting to take back His blessings or what He promised us. Even when we walk away, He remains. Our human minds can't even conceive that kind of love, but it is real.

After several weeks of private meetings with Kristen, I challenged her to read a book with me, *Emotionally Healthy Spirituality* by Pete Scazzero.[22] It took several meetings to forge the walls of her heart, but slowly, the Holy Spirit began to chip away at them. Sometimes, healing is instantaneous, and sometimes, healing is a process. What matters is that we commit to it.

I watched God do a beautiful work in Kristen. She's been on our full-time staff team since 2019. In that time, I have seen hope restored, her heart healed, shame destroyed, and purpose reignited. She and her husband are raising two amazing boys. She is passing on to her family and the world around her the freedom she has found. She knows her worth, walks in God-confidence, and is changing lives from a personal place. I am so proud of her. When God assigns worth to us, nothing and no one can diminish our value. The intruder of unworthiness is blocked by knowing where your value is derived. It's through Jesus!

1) **Investigate Your Heart** (Honesty): Is the intruder of unworthiness causing me to live at a place of lower value in any area of my life?
2) **Challenge Your Beliefs** (Truth): Lamentations 4:2; Romans 8:18; Genesis 1:27; Romans 11:25-29.
3) **Set and Enforce Your Boundaries** (Wisdom): I will remind myself that God alone is able to define my value. I will keep my

---
22 Pete Scazzero, *Emotionally Healthy Spirituality: It's Impossible to Be Spiritually Mature While Remaining Emotionally Immature* (Grand Rapids, MI: Zondervan, 2017).

life free from shame. I will do everything I can to live a life worthy of the price Christ paid on the cross for me.

INVADER OF UNFORGIVENESS

Hurt has touched everyone who is old enough to understand pain. This invader does severe damage because it disguises itself as justified. Unforgiveness places the blame on another person or situation rather than requiring you to look inside yourself! Unforgiveness steals the joy and peace right out of your heart! It often brings with it the offspring of a victim mindset. Unforgiveness stiffens your growth and hinders your ability to see clearly. When our hearts welcome unforgiveness and bitterness, our lives are full of chaos, pain, and mistrust! Sometimes, the pain is deep. What happened to you felt out of your control. Holding on to unforgiveness can feel warranted and safe, but it is a death sentence. No one knows this better than Julia, one of my amazing girls at The Avenue:

Shame and unforgiveness demand isolation. Shame commands that we live within the confined lines of "no one can ever know," and every day, we take up residence in that neighborhood. Unforgiveness locks the door that shame constructed. And the enemy of our faith adds another brick along the long wall of bitterness. Unforgiveness builds a wall that feels like Jericho. Massive walls, with giants, we are just not ready to slay. Your promise is beyond the Jericho walls. My battle with Jericho began when I was nine years old. Brick by brick, I built a wall and it was when I was twenty-seven that I would start my journey to my promised land.

From the outside, our family had everything you could ask for. My mom was a stay-at-home mom until my siblings and I were all in school. My dad worked, and we grew up next door to my grandparents. We played sports, enjoyed social gatherings . . . all the things! The enemy doesn't destroy a foundation overnight, however. He's slow, silent, and calculated. He waits patiently for the right time to strike, and he has no limits on who he will use to destroy those whom God loves (not even a nine-year-old girl). You have to first identify the events that have caused a trauma response in your brain and body before you can move on to any other part of finding freedom.

There are two defining moments for me: one when I was twelve years old and the other when I was eighteen. Yes, many other events in my life added to my Jericho walls, but those events were a by-product of the two main defining moments. It is important that you know the difference between the roots and the limbs that grow from them.

My father began using drugs before I was born. I'm currently forty-one years old. So, mathematically, that's a long time. When I was nine, my dad used them for eleven years. He unintentionally developed an addiction. I mean, nobody sets out on that course. It's a hard road to turn off once you drive it for so long. He had earned a full-ride scholarship to college to play football, but a knee injury eliminated him from playing and he dropped out of college. He became a long-distance truck driver and began using speed as a means to stay awake. That would be the catalyst that would send him into a lifetime of downward spiraling. Impaired judgment, financial irresponsibility, absenteeism, and the list goes on.

Of course, it doesn't start that way. But keeping it all together was simply impossible. When I was in third grade, a family member who lived in our home began dating a man who, at best, had highly questionable character. When they started seeing each other, he was already facing severe charges for a recent crime. In the beginning, his behavior was not blatantly violent or threatening. It would be a while—almost three years—before the man's true self would be exposed as I would wake up one morning being molested by this man—a man who had gained my trust and groomed me for this moment. I'll never forget how, in an instant, I felt different. Ashamed. Scared. Confused. I remember later sitting in our little kitchen, terrified to tell my mom and yet terrified to say nothing. It would be another fifteen years before I realized this moment was my root number one.

At the same time, my dad's drug addiction took the only home I had ever known. All of this completely changed the course of my life and set me on a completely unknown path, one that would be the complete opposite of anything I had ever known. It would be another six years of hell before my parents divorced. At that time, the man who molested me went to jail for the crime for which he was facing charges. When he was released, the abuse resumed and continued until I was in high school. My abuser introduced me to drugs and alcohol, which became a daily part of my life until I was twenty-seven years old. Every. Day.

When I was eighteen, a senior in high school, my mom reached a day where she could no longer take the cycle of addiction that consumed our home. She picked up the phone and told my dad that it was over. A couple of months later, he showed up at our house and told me that he never wanted to have anything to do with me ever again. I reminded him too much of my mom. It has been twenty-two years since he spoke those words, and our relationship has never been the same. At that moment, I decided no one would ever make me feel that way, ever again. My father's words to me were root number two.

Unforgiveness lives at the base of those unexposed roots, and it will make your heart sick. Unforgiveness will cause you to guard your heart in an unhealthy way. It robs you of the life lived in Christ Jesus. It causes roots of bitterness, offense, jealousy, and distraction, to name a few. Generous forgiveness is not easy but necessary for victory. The enemy will cause you to believe that if you forgive the offense, you condone the offense. But forgiveness is crucial to your victory. It's not a choice; it's a requirement. When thoughts of bitterness and anger begin to rise in your heart, take those thoughts captive and submit them to Christ! Forgiveness brings freedom.

Julia is free and walks others through healing daily as she serves on our pastoral staff team. She is strong, composed, driven, and hard-working. She's incredible. Seeing her raise two beautiful miracle daughters and succeed in marriage to her husband, Matt, proves that forgiveness releases blessings. Her words show how much God can do when we surrender our story to Him. Julia's story is difficult to process, but unfortunately, more common than you'd think. According to National Statistics of Abuse from the National Children's Alliance, more than 600,000 children are abused or neglected every year. That abuse can be physical, emotional, sexual, or psychological. That number is just the reported and confirmed cases. In reality, we know that a lot of cases go unreported. Of those cases reported, two-thirds of them involve sexual abuse.[23] If you've been hurt, please know you are not alone.

---

[23] "National Child Abuse Statistics from NCA," *National Children's Alliance*, 4 Mar. 2024, www.nationalchildrensalliance.org/media-room/national-statistics-on-child-abuse/.

> ## *Forgiveness isn't a single act; it must be a permanent heart posture.*

The way to stand against this invader is simple, but it can be challenging. Remember how much you've been forgiven, and extend that same forgiveness to others! Christ tells us that if we don't forgive, we ourselves cannot be forgiven. Matthew 6:14-15 says, "For if you forgive other people when they sin against you, your heavenly Father will also forgive you. But if you do not forgive others their sins, your Father will not forgive your sins." Forgive, no matter what a person has said or done to you. No matter how deep the offense, forgive. Thank God for His grace and mercy on your life, and then extend it to others. There is so much freedom in that act of obedience. Extending forgiveness doesn't mean you have to subject yourself to continual hurt. You can enforce boundaries. But real forgiveness releases the wrong and sets that person free, setting you free in return.

Don't rehearse the wrong that was done to you, and don't come up with excuses for why it's okay not to forgive! Choose forgiveness every day! Forgiveness isn't a single act; it must be a permanent heart posture. Expect people to hurt, betray, and mistreat you, and then decide in advance that you will always forgive. After twenty-plus years in ministry, I have some experience in this category! People will cut you deeply. Forgive them. People will mistreat you. Forgive them. People will talk about you, and you will never get to defend yourself. Forgive them. Forgiveness must be a daily choice so that your heart stays free. The heart invader of unforgiveness is blocked by a heart postured to forgive!

1) **Investigate Your Heart** (Honesty): Search your heart for offenses that you have held on to. Are there people or situations you need to forgive or receive forgiveness from the Lord?
2) **Challenge Your Beliefs** (Truth): Romans 12:9-21; 2 Corinthians 2:3-11; Matthew 6:5-14
3) **Set and Enforce Your Boundaries** (Wisdom): I will keep my heart from holding unforgiveness. I will choose daily to release the wrong done to me—past, present, and future. I will keep healthy boundaries in relationships so I do not invite offense into my life.

INVADERS OF ANXIETY AND DEPRESSION

These two come to steal our joy and freedom. I am a pastor with a degree in counseling. That has its advantages as we meet with and counsel people. We are mind, body, and spirit. When we assist believers with mental health, we cannot forget that. I believe in spiritual warfare. I believe in freedom. I believe in prayer. However, a physical or chemical imbalance can trigger an emotional or mental reaction. What this means is to guard your heart against anxiety and depression, you must remember to think body, soul, and spirit.

Most of us remember the times during and after the worldwide COVID-19 pandemic. Living through that as a pastor was incredibly difficult. We were seeking God and leaning into other leaders daily for wisdom. Our goal was to ensure the church remained strong and healthy, and that when it was "over," our community had us to lean on for strength. Thankfully, we accomplished both things, but it came at a price. I have often tried to put words behind the emotions of that season. But in my head, all I can see is the scene from Home Alone where the thieves are trying to break into the house, and they go from one disaster to another. That's what the years during and after the pandemic were like—one disaster after another.

Though its effects are still around today, the COVID-19 season for us, as leaders, lasted two years. We quickly discovered that things were changing daily, and people needed peace. We have an incredible team of leaders serving around us, so staying connected with our people wasn't difficult. We adopted so many great new ways of doing things. We solved problems we never anticipated we would need to solve. We wept with people who lost friends and family. We celebrated when our people were well and healed. We tried to honor our government (federal and state) to follow all the mandates. We remained neutral while passions and anger flared over the issues of masks and vaccinations. We stood with our brothers and sisters of color to fight racism. We endured intense political agendas from both sides and still taught the unchanging Word of God every week. Like everyone else, we overused the words "social distancing" and "quarantine" to ensure everyone felt protected. We cleaned more than we ever had to ensure we were thoughtful of everyone when we gathered. We endured social media pandemonium and educated our people to remain Christlike through it. We saw some families change for the better as being at home was mandated and encouraged. We watched other families divide and disagree. People fall away from God and the church. We closed our building to in-person services for seven weeks and chose to go online only. Our online campus grew the church larger than ever, and the reach became global. People were still getting saved weekly, and we were finding ways to connect with them.

We experienced the most extreme mental, physical, and emotional conditions our world had experienced up to that point in my lifetime. (And you did, too.) We did all of that while leading thousands of people simultaneously. Our goal was to carry everyone safely through it in a way that honored and pleased God. Once we were clear, my body, mind, and emotions tanked.

I had never heard of it before that time, but I now know it was adrenal exhaustion. Remember how I told you earlier that the mind and heart communicate? The amygdala is a small command center in the center of your brain; it has a big job. The heart sends signals to this part of your brain about how it feels. The brain then processes all the emotions and sends signals to the adrenal gland.[24] The adrenal gland releases adrenaline and cortisol hormones into the bloodstream, creating a physical response: racing heart, fatigue, sleeplessness, nervousness, food cravings, etc. In prolonged stress states, this disrupts the brain's ability to process thoughts and balance moods. When this happens, our bodies stay stuck in fight, flight, or freeze mode, leading to adrenal fatigue. Clinical research shows that people with depression and anxiety have an overactive amygdala.[25] Please do some research if that interests you. That was a physical and emotional response in my body. It happened; I lived it. I had to treat my body with vitamins and find new ways to process emotions and stress.

There was also a spiritual attack at work along with the physical attacks. I was experiencing crazy demonic attacks; the enemy would whisper that he was going to take my life. I struggled falling asleep most nights for the first time in my life. I would fall asleep praying and wake up praying. I was in my Word; before I would even get out of bed, I spoke Scripture over my mind and heart. I was in my secret place of worship. I was prayed for, loved on, and cared for by the most amazing friends and family. Here is what I have discovered. Sometimes, the weapons that protect your heart will be forged and wielded in the hands of others. New friendships were formed that

---

[24] "Amygdala," *Cleveland Clinic*, accessed June 15, 2024, https://my.clevelandclinic.org/health/body/24894-amygdala.

[25] Ann Kearns, "Adrenal Fatigue: What Causes It?," *Mayo Clinic*, 10 Apr. 2024, https://www.mayoclinic.org/diseases-conditions/addisons-disease/expert-answers/adrenal-fatigue/faq-20057906.

season, and I allowed a select few into my struggle. What kept me going was knowing that seasons don't last forever. I knew the attack would leave the same way it came—SUDDENLY. I would do all I could in the natural and believe in God for the supernatural.

Sometimes, God removes the intruders of anxiety and depression out of your way. Sometimes, He will give you extra strength as you fight and defeat them. BUT ALL THE time, His promise endures. Through that season, I learned so many things, but here is the part I want you to hear: you can love God, be full of the Spirit, and experience feelings of anxiety and depression. Your job is to set your life up so those intruders do not come in and stay! Philippians 4:6-7 (emphasis added) tells us how:

> *Do not be anxious about anything, but in every situation,* by **prayer** *and* **petition,** *with* **thanksgiving,** *present your* **requests** *to God. And* **the peace of God,** *which transcends all understanding,* **will guard your hearts** *and minds* **in Christ** *Jesus.*

I can feel a lot of things, but I don't have to give those feelings ownership.

The first half of that verse is a command with actions and steps on your part. The second half is a promise attached to the obedience of doing your part. The promise is that He will guard our hearts if we walk through the process. Here are the steps:

1) **Refuse to "own" anxiety.** Do not BE anxious about anything. Being and feeling are two different things. If I say I feel rich riding in a nice car, that means the car has produced feelings of wealth. That doesn't make me wealthy. But, if I say, "I am rich riding in a nice car," I have just owned the feeling and allowed it to define me. There is a difference between "feeling" and "being." Feeling anxious is descriptive and factual. It is a feeling. I don't know about you, but I have a lot of feelings. Some feelings are valid, and some are not. We cannot put our trust in our feelings. What happens next is the step that a lot of people miss. Being anxious is owning and identifying things in a definitive way. I can feel a lot of things, but I don't have to give those feelings ownership. I don't have to allow feelings to define me. That is what the scripture means. Don't let anxiety become your identity! Instead of "being'" anxious, run to the One who owns your heart.

2) **Pray.** This is connection. When I have anxious feelings, I take them to the One I trust. When I do, this signifies He owns my heart. I take my feelings to Him. He can help me guard my heart from allowing the intruders of anxiety and depression to set up camp in my life. Prayer is where I draw the line in the sand: He is my source that owns the source (my heart). I will always run to Him!

3) **Petition.** Request an answer. This is where prayer goes deep. We pour out the issue in detail and then ask Him to answer. Sometimes, His answer points us to the solution (work we can do), and other times, His answer IS the solution (His hand in the situation).

4) **Thanksgiving.** Gratitude is an attitude of the heart that should always accompany our prayers. Cypress Counseling Center in Ann Arbor, Michigan, conducted an extensive study on

gratitude. They found, "The impact of gratitude on the brain is long-lasting. Besides enhancing empathy and self-love, gratitude significantly impacts bodily response functions and psychological conditions such as anxiety, stress, and depression."[26] Could it be that God, who created the mind, body, and soul, knew that this was part of the remedy to our freedom? Of course, His Word is an intentional roadmap. Gratitude! List your blessings, and thank God for them. Spend time reflecting on all He has given and done for you.

5) **Requests.** Tell Him exactly what you need. Be specific and definite. I like to thank Him for already giving me freedom. In other words, before He answers, I will thank Him in advance. He has already provided what I need. I want Him to know that I know He is already working!

Scripture is clear: He will do His thing when we do the things outlined in Scripture. He will guard our hearts and minds with peace. It's His promise to us! I have learned that as long as the peace of God goes with me, I can go anywhere and face anything. That is a promise that is worth walking out. I don't know how long the season of suffering will be for you and I don't have to. But I do know who is in control of the seasons. Just keep walking through the feelings. Lean into others for support. It would be best if you did not walk this season alone. Grow in the knowledge of who He is to you. And trust that He has something in that season for you to learn.

Our youth pastor, Mackenzie, recently had her first baby. Like a lot of women, postpartum was difficult. Mackenzie and I met and discussed the difficulty of this transition. Mackenzie is a beautiful momma. I love her sweet smile and deep heart for Jesus. She and her hubby, Wes, are a blessing; their sweet son is also. Because I have

---

26 "The Link between Practicing Gratitude and Reduced Anxiety," *Cypress Counseling Center, P.C.*, accessed April 16, 2024, https://www.cypresscounselingcenter.com/blog/the-link-between-practicing-gratitude-and-reduced-anxiety/.

been where they are, I can speak to it from the other side. When you walk through it, it feels like things might never level out. Emotions feel insurmountable, your mind races all the time, and the demands of taking care of a baby take your physical health to the limit. Because I have walked it, I can confidently tell her to keep walking. When you are in these hard seasons, make sure you pray, petition, and have a heart of gratitude and confidence, and He will answer. You must do the physical, spiritual, and emotional heart checks. But at the end of the day always acknowledge God and the season, and let Him know you are listening and obeying. Obedience has the power to shift seasons. I need Him to know I am postured to learn, and I am listening. I don't want to spend one unnecessary self-inflicted moment in this place. The peace of God blocks the intruders of anxiety and depression.

1) **Investigate Your Heart** (Honesty): Am I feeling anxiety and depression or owning anxiety and depression?
2) **Challenge Your Beliefs** (Truth): Philippians 4:6-7; Psalms 94:19; Matthew 6:25-33
3) **Set and Enforce Your Boundaries** (Wisdom): I will learn how to feel without allowing the feeling to own me. I will pray, petition, be grateful, and make my requests known. I will trust and walk through the season instead of getting stuck.

INVADER OF APATHY

One of P. T. Barnum's biggest life values was passion, creator of the Barnum & Bailey Circus. He said, "Comfort is the enemy of progress."[27] He spent his life proving he would not be caught in that trap. Passion like his was rare in the 1800s. The world around him did all it could to derail his thinking. His life was so spectacular that the 2018

---

27 P.T. Barnum Quotes," *Goodreads*, accessed April 18, 2024, https://www.goodreads.com/author/quotes/201036.P_T_Barnum.

movie *The Greatest Showman*[28] was produced. His story of passion is still being told today. Apathy comes to steal your passion. Apathy is indifference. It is a lack of emotion and drive. Apathy comes for many different reasons. This is an invader most people in the Western world will face head-on.

As people of faith, we find this especially dangerous. Faith and our relationship with Christ should never become comfortable. We should always grow. We should always work on becoming more like Christ. We should all avoid feeling good enough, bright enough, or mature enough. Hebrews 12:1 speaks to us about our walk of faith, and the writer compares our relationship with Christ and growing in faith to a race. It says, "Let us strip off every weight that slows us down, especially the sin that so easily trips us up. And let us run with endurance the race God has set before us" (NLT). Apathy is a weight that rests on you, causing you to sit down and stop progressing. But just like in a race, if you sit down, you will lose! There is no "good enough" in a race. You win, or you lose. I love the visual of a race. It speaks of intentionality.

My son is a cross-country runner; his love for running is inspirational. Watching him has taught me so much about perseverance, pushing for more, discipline, and endurance. Late in his middle school years, he decided he loved running. We were those parents who encouraged our children to try every sport to find the one they loved. Being on a team teaches you so many lessons! (I could talk about team mentality for a long time, but I will move on.) Once they found their sport, we encouraged them to invest time and energy into making improvements. By the time Judah was in eighth grade, we could see that running would be his sport. He became hungry for success, loved running, and was good at it.

---

28 Michael Gracey, *The Greatest Showman* (December 20, 2017; Los Angeles, CA: 20th Century Studios).

In his freshman year of high school, his team made it to state. He was the sixth man on his varsity team! Making it to state is a big deal for a freshman in high school! What was even better than making it to the state finals was that the victory made him hungry to succeed even more. He stepped up his practicing and running in the off-season to improve his time and build his endurance. By his sophomore year, he made the all-regional team and his second state appearance, running third on his team. He is training for his junior year, and his times have already improved. His goal this year is to place at state, and I believe he can do it. That is what passion looks like. Passion will keep you driven for more. It will never let you settle for mediocrity. That is what 1 Corinthians 9:24 means when it says, "Don't you realize that in a race everyone runs, but only one person gets the prize? So run to win!" (NLT)

God has set His followers to win. Winners don't settle for average. Winners don't possess a "just enough" or "I'll never" mentality. They don't expect the award to be handed to them for no effort. Winners are passionate about finishing first. It's that type of passion that we should apply to our faith. Passion should fuel us to grow and push us to pursue Christ and all He has for our lives. Apathy is described in Revelation 3:15-16 (NLT), "I know all the things you do, that you are neither hot nor cold. I wish that you were one or the other! But since you are like lukewarm water, neither hot nor cold, I will spit you out of my mouth!" Our apathy makes God sick! Love God, pursue all He has for you, or hate Him and choose darkness. The Kingdom of God is either/or, not both/and. Spiritual indifference will destroy you. Apathy will remove you from the race. Where apathy is accepted, passion will be rejected. Guard your heart. The invader of apathy is blocked by passion and a desire to win.

1) **Investigate Your Heart** (Honesty): Search my heart, God. Show me if there is any pride in me.
2) **Challenge Your Beliefs** (Truth): Philippians 3:12-14; Hebrews 12:1; 1 Corinthians 5:25-27; James 4:10; Proverbs 18:12
3) **Set and Enforce Your Boundaries** (Wisdom): I will maintain a humble heart by asking God to search my heart continually. I will serve others with honor and humility. I will remember that I am to be like Christ, who came not to be served but to serve.

INVADER OF PRIDE

God hates pride. Why, you ask? Pride destroys all it controls. Pride created the devil. It was pride that turned Lucifer, the son of the morning, into Satan. Ezekiel 28 and Isaiah 14:13-16 describe Lucifer before, during, and after the fall of pride. Those chapters share that pride caused him to fall, be thrown to Earth, and lose everything God had given him. Pride was also the downfall of the human race. In Genesis, Satan came to Eve with the fruit. The taste of the fruit didn't tempt her. The garden was full of all kinds of fruit. It was Satan who tempted her when he said, "Eat this, and you will be like God." He used the same thing to bring down Adam and Eve that he used that caused him to fall. It worked then, and it is still working today. We were born with pride, ego, and selfishness in our hearts (Mark 7:21), which is human nature. I hate to tell you this, but it's true. No one has to teach you to be selfish and prideful; it comes naturally. Pride is the chief cause of misery in every area of your life. It leads to all sin and destruction. Pride is the leading value in Satan's kingdom. Knowing this is Satan's vice, it is appropriate to stay far away from pride. Pride comes to destroy your heart. God is against pride because it defies God. How can we stay alert so we do not fall into the sin of pride? Simple—we remember our foundation.

John 15:5 tells us, "I am the vine; you are the branches. If you remain in me and I in you, you will bear much fruit; apart from me you can do nothing." In that moment, it is as if He was taking the disciples back to the garden of Eden in a way. It was His way of saying, "Don't make the same mistakes. Don't let pride cause you to forget that I am the source. If you choose pride over connectivity with Me, you will see the end is only death." The only way to keep the intruder of pride out of your life is to foster a heart posture of humility. Genuine humility comes from a heart positioned below Christ. One that recognizes He is God, and you are not. Remember, your life flows from your heart. A heart positioned in humility will lead to a life lived in humility. If that is your desire, then there are some efficient ways to keep this invader at bay. The shortlist: prayer, the Word, and worship. (We will break these down together in a future chapter.) Remind yourself: pride is Satan's currency; you want nothing to do with it. The intruder of pride is defeated by a heart of humility.

1) **Investigate Your Heart** (Honesty): Are there areas where I have let apathy create a place of comfort in my life?
2) **Challenge Your Beliefs** (Truth): James 3:13; 1 Peter 5:5-6.
3) **Set and Enforce Your Boundaries** (Wisdom): I will remember He is God, and I am not. I will keep my heart free from pride through prayer, Reading God's Word, and having times of worship daily. I will remind myself that apart from Him, I can do nothing.

SOUND THE ALARM

We have just done some difficult investigating. I am confident the Lord has helped you see where your heart has been compromised. The alarm of your heart has sounded, and together, we have applied honesty and truth. I am confident in your ability to take what the Lord has shown you and secure the boundaries of your heart. Tighten up security and ensure all the windows and doors of your heart remain locked to potential intruders. You've already decided that your heart is worth the investment, or you would not have made it this far! You aren't afraid of hard work. You have confronted the enemy. Truth has brought healing. The truth will continue to bring healing. And you don't have to fall victim to those intruders again.

The enemy has been exposed and defeated. He was a kidnapper trying to hold a life captive, only to realize that the ransom had already been paid in full. Jesus has come for your heart. He is crazy in love with you. The moment you called on Him for help, He was already there. No matter how painful the journey of your heart has been, He has never left you. He is our Creator, and His plans for us are so good. His love is beyond understanding. He heals and restores even when the wounds are self-inflicted. He redeems us for His use. He offers us freedom so that we can live a life beyond imagination. He is faithful in walking this journey with us. He is kind when we don't deserve it. He is the truth among all the lies. He is our joy, and that joy is our strength. He is forever ours, our great reward. Oh, yes, He is all this and so much more! All He asks is that we would willingly return to Him our hearts. Can you even fathom all of that?

PRAYER OF COMMITMENT

Father, thank You that You have never left me. You have been with me through everything; I see it now. Please continue to make this journey clear. Help me be on guard against any intruder seeking to invade my heart. Remind me that You are there, and give me the courage to address any invaders hiding in my heart's shadows. My heart is Yours; I love you. AMEN!

HEART ON FIRE

"My heart grew hot within me. While I meditated, the fire burned; then I spoke with my tongue."
—PSALMS 39:3

We live in the most beautiful landscape in the United States: East Tennessee, amidst the majestic Smoky Mountains. I have lived in many places, but this place is the best. The scenery and the people are second to none. The Smoky Mountains, various national and state parks, and lakes around us attract thousands of tourists yearly. I can't say that I blame them; it's spectacular.

In November 2016, our area was under a severe drought. On November 23, 2016, a wildfire began to burn in the Great Smoky Mountain National Park. Wildfires aren't uncommon. The determination was that they would create a 400-acre containment area and allow the fire to burn out. In hindsight, it was that decision where a bad situation turned worse than anyone could have imagined. By November 28, our area was experiencing hurricane-force winds. The wind was picking up sparks of fire and throwing them through the surrounding forests. The fire spread quickly, and the wind made the spread unpredictable. Gatlinburg Skypark reported:

> By December 12, the fires had claimed at least 14 lives and burned more than 17,900 acres (27 square miles), making it one of the largest natural disasters in the history of Tennessee. At least 14,000 people had to be evacuated, and over 2,400 buildings were damaged or destroyed.[29]

The fires burned thirty-five miles from where we live, and we felt the magnitude of their destruction. The atmosphere filled with smoke, and ash blew into our area for days. That wildfire has been the deadliest wildfire in the eastern US since the Great Fires of 1947 in Maine. Fire is a powerful force of nature. It consumes, bringing with it heat and light that is undeniable. The atmosphere plays the most critical role in fire management. I learned so much about fire when we faced all the days surrounding the event in 2016. An interesting thing I discovered at that time was a "controlled burn."

A controlled burn is when a forest fire is planned. Controlled burns, called "prescribed fires," have been skillfully planned. At the time of the fires of 2016, this was the first I had learned about this process. However, I discovered that a controlled burn is a common occurrence. These types of fires are needed and beneficial for forests. The purpose: to burn up dead trees, old shrubbery, and weeds so new plants and vegetation can grow. There are also numerous plants and animal habitats that are dependent on fire to survive. A prescribed fire will always have an objective. A burn plan is required before anything can begin. The plan is set upon the atmosphere needed, the fuel that will burn, and the boundaries of the fire's location.[30]

Ultimately, the controlled fire equals gain. When it's done correctly, the result of this type of fire is increase. Vegetation, wildlife,

---

[29] "The Gatlinburg Wildfires," *Gatlinburg SkyPark*, accessed June 1, 2024, https://www.gatlinburgskypark.com/gatlinburg-wildfires.

[30] "Prescribed Fire," *Tennessee Wildland Fire*, accessed May 10, 2024, https://www.tn.gov/tnwildlandfire/prescribed-fire.html.

economy, and professional development among the firefighters will all experience significant gains. When I envision forest fire, the gain is not my first thought. When I think of fire, I envision destruction and devastation. Incredibly, intentionality is the only factor determining if it will end in gain or devastation.

Our hearts are the same way. By now, you've learned your heart is the source and central to life. You have decided that you have to take responsibility for the source. You have seen the echo of your life tell on your heart. And you have identified heart invaders and determined ways to guard against them. To see your heart grow in new life and be a source of gain, God wants to start a controlled burn in your heart. That is an intentional fire by a purposeful God. He knows the objective and what needs to burn away so you can experience life in Him like never before. He is the fire, and our hearts are the landscape.

FIRE IN THE BIBLE

Fire is a transformational symbol in Scripture that is both powerful and layered in purpose. The first time fire was introduced in the Bible was when Adam and Eve were ejected from the Garden of Eden in Genesis 3. An angel with a sword of fire was there to block the entrance back into the perfect place. The last time fire is mentioned is in Revelation 21:7-8 when all unbelievers will one day be cast into the lake of fire. Fire is mentioned around five hundred times throughout the entire Bible.[31] The defining contexts of these encounters are vast and powerful. I could spend all day breaking down the Scriptures and showing the incredible nature of God depicted through each interaction with fire. What is crucial for us to note is what fire represents: God's Spirit is near. Each mention of fire had so many meanings: to signify His presence resting in a place, the receiving of a sacrifice,

---

31 "Fire in the Bible: An in-Depth Look at Its First Mention and Profound Significance," *Christian Pure*, 27 May, 2024, https://christianpure.com/learn/fire-in-the-bible/.

providing light in the desert, judgment for sin, or speaking from a bush. He appeared as tongues of fire to empower His followers, and His eyes are described as fire in Revelation.

> *He is intentional with fire because He is the Fire.*

No matter the context, we see God. We see His Spirit. We can stand in awe and wonder. We serve a powerful and creative God. He is the fire. That is why when we surrender our lives to Him, His Spirit begins working in us. In 1 Peter 1, the apostle Peter tells believers that our "shaping" to become more like Christ is like being purified in the refiner's fire. Fire is essential to us as believers. But the common denominator, no matter the story, is that He is intentional with fire because He is the Fire. Fire has a purpose. It always has, and it always will. Fire is His presence, lighting the way to accomplish what needs to be accomplished. What a holy, awe-inspiring, and incredible God we serve! He was the fire. He is the fire.

We can thank Him in gratitude because He will always be the fire. He is burning in the hearts of all who put their hope in Him. As we work through a heart of fire, I want you to picture a mighty, powerful, loving God. He cares so deeply about the condition of your heart. He loves us way too much to leave us as we were when we came to Him. He isn't a manufactured fire. His flame will never grow dim. He will never get tired of His children gathering around His light. He is honored when we ask Him to make our heart's atmosphere more like His. He is overjoyed when we surrender to His plan and follow

His prescription for our hearts to burn. He is glorified among His people when we submit to godly wisdom and accountability. Open your heart and invite Him to come and burn in you. I love the words of a simple worship chorus written by Will Raegan that says: "Set a fire down in my soul that I can't contain and I can't control." He is the fire, and He is what our hearts need. He is what our heart should desire, more of Him in every part of us.

ELEMENTS OF CONTROLLED BURN

God desires that His Spirit consume every heart. We are supposed to be fire starters in the world and flame keepers in our lives! Remember, fire burning in us = the Holy Spirit alive in our hearts. Fire brings the passion to grow in relationship with Him. Everyone who has committed to a life following Jesus must have a fire burning in their hearts. Anytime His fire consumes us, you know He is up to something great. Our prescribed burn depends on the needs and state of our hearts for each of us. Because we are all unique, we must determine our heart's needs. Although our plans are different, they will all need three things to let Him burn intentionally: atmosphere, prescription, and boundaries.

1) **Atmosphere:**

The atmosphere is the predominant temperature, tone, or mood of a place. The current atmosphere of your heart is determined by the things you've walked through up to this point. Let's look at a quick summary of the ideas and principles we have discussed thus far:

- The heart is central to everything.
- The need for a new heart is accomplished by developing a relationship with Christ.
- Self-care and discipline are accomplished by taking responsibility to own the gate of our hearts.

- Think-feel-choose is based on internal beliefs and a value system that exposes and transforms our thought patterns and life perspectives.
- We are only able to change when we crush our excuses.
- We thoroughly self-evaluate when we acknowledge that our lives are an echo of our hearts.
- The echo cycle of your heart is Source → Sound → Symphony.
- We identify the heart invaders that ravage our hearts, we repent, and we guard our hearts from all future intruders.

Our hearts have a preferred atmosphere—an optimal performance setting. We must consider all of these things as we discover our current atmosphere and determine where it needs to be.

A fight happens at some point in every home around the world. It is a fight over the thermostat! Everyone in the home desires a different living temperature. In our house, year-round, it is set to 69 degrees Fahrenheit. Cold is my husband's preferred setting, and I go with it since I can add layers. Much like the fight for the TV remote, I pick my battles (lol). However, something we have in common is our nightly exchange of disapproval regarding the temperature.

My statement is, "It's freezing in here," evidenced by the icicles hanging from the end of my nose and the extremities on my hands and feet that have lost feeling! The ideal temperature for me would be 71 degrees year-round. My husband says, "It's so hot in here." This is evidenced by his persistent fanning and the beads of sweat collecting on his face. He would love it if I agreed to keep the thermostat at 67 degrees. So, we agree to meet in the middle. I know this is a funny comparison. We all, indeed, feel and process things differently. Our hearts are the same way—they are different. We all experience the world in a different heart climate.

Weather is an important factor when planning a controlled burn. The atmosphere determines how the fire behaves and can mean the complete success or failure of the burn. Our hearts are identical. We all have different atmospheres, but we all need fire. To make this burn successful, we must first start with the atmosphere our hearts are in today. We have discussed and listed factors that determine our atmosphere: family history, personality traits, and heart invaders (amount, depth of invasion, plan to guard). Our relationship with Christ is vital. It's not about being good enough; it's about wisdom and understanding. We all know where we want and need to go, but each of us will be on a different road to get there.

Because we all start in different places, there is no cookie-cutter answer as to the heart atmosphere we need in order to ignite the fire. The good news is that the atmosphere will be easy to discover by looking at the aforementioned factors and doing our groundwork. The goal for all of us is to get the atmosphere of our hearts to a place of freedom to receive the fire. If the atmosphere of our hearts isn't ready when the fire comes, we will smother it and risk it going out.

For a fire to ignite, wind and fuel must mix, and the atmosphere must foster the burn. If it is too dry, it burns too fast and furious; if it is too humid, it burns too slow and unpredictably. There is an atmosphere that is perfect for a controlled burn. The landscape, the debris to be burned, and where it burns all affect the atmosphere. The timeliness and temperature of the burn are determined by the amount of debris it has to get through.

Here are some things we can do to make sure the atmosphere of our hearts will burn the way God desires:

- **Spiritual Renewal**: Put Christ first. Make time for prayer, the Word, and worship. Connect to a life-giving body of Christ.
- **Thought Renewal**: Nurture positive, balanced thinking that fosters a constructive and healthy outlook on every area of life.
- **Emotional Regulation**: Effectively manage your emotions and ensure you express them in a healthy way.

- **Social Support**: Build strong, supportive relationships that provide emotional sustenance and a sense of belonging with good boundaries.
- **Physical Well-Being**: Participate in regular activities that nurture physical, mental, and emotional health (exercise, prayer, and personal hobbies).
- **Life Balance**: Adopt a well-rounded lifestyle centered around Christ. This balance should include time for work, rest, play, and personal growth.
- **Gratitude and Mindfulness**: Engage in practices that focus on the present moment and appreciation for all your blessings.
- **Personal Values and Beliefs**: Generate a set of values and beliefs that guide actions and provide a sense of purpose to your life.

We must evaluate the atmosphere of our hearts daily. Remember, this is a marathon, not a sprint. Our goal should be an atmosphere that stays in optimal fire mode each day. I am thankful to have witnessed many atmospheres change in people's lives.

A lady named Chris called the church and requested a meeting with me. She had been coming to the church with her husband for six months. They were newly married and had just moved to the area from North Carolina. Up to this point, our interactions had been minimal. What I knew about her was that she was intelligent and super friendly. When she smiled, the kindness in her heart could be seen in her eyes. I was happy to have the opportunity to sit down and spend some time with her. I love to hear people's stories. Knowing where people come from and what they have been through is essential to understanding their hearts.

The day she walked into my office, I experienced something unexpected. She walked through the door, and we hugged and talked briefly. She began to share her story with me. Chris began to cry, and what happened next was written in my 2021 planner for that day (yes, I kept it!). I hadn't heard her story yet, but the Holy Spirit whispered, "I sent her here for my church. *She will work for you one day.*" (Those are the moments when I am thankful for the fire of the Holy Spirit.) I pray that I always stay sensitive to His voice and that He never stops the whispers. I wrote those words down but didn't say anything to anyone about them.

Chris had been in ministry with her first husband; they pastored a church together. She had extensive experience working in the financial field, and she had an incredibly successful consulting business in North Carolina. Chris shared about her two grown daughters and beamed with pride as she expressed their accomplishments. She talked about her life experience before her recent pain. Chris shared through tears that she and her husband had divorced due to his unfaithfulness several years prior. Chris's story had gripped my heart. When you listen to someone's heart through their words, you better understand who she is inside. Looking into her eyes, I could see pain. My heart went out to her. The more Chris shared in sincerity, the more I understood the complexity of her situation. A while after her divorce, she met a wonderful man. They married, and she moved here to start a new life with him.

Betrayal and mistrust by the people we love the most have a way of drastically shifting the atmosphere of our hearts. It can cause the wind to stop blowing. Mistrust creates debris that can take over the beauty we once enjoyed. Before you know it, so much needs to be addressed, and you need help figuring out where to begin. This is the point where some people get stuck, but not Chris. She communicated everything with so much grace and forgiveness. As I listened, I thought, could I be that gracious in her situation? After some time sharing where she had been, something shifted.

Suddenly, I didn't hear pain as much as I heard gratitude. She began to talk about where she was now. Chris shared how grateful she was to be in this place. She had never entered a spirit-filled church before coming to The Avenue. And it was changing her life. At that moment, she told me, "I know I have a long way to go, but I am grateful to have a new life." Then she said, "However I can serve, I am more than willing to do it." She was extremely humble about how much knowledge she had in finance.

Here is what I know about the atmosphere of our lives: when we choose to take steps to change it, God is faithful in meeting us in the middle. It was clear at that moment that God sent Chris to us, first and foremost, so that we could help change the atmosphere of her life, but also so He could, in turn, use her in the atmosphere of His Kingdom. Over the next year, I watched God shift everything for Chris. He used her gifts to lead others. She was never stingy with her story and was always quick to share how good God had been. Within a year, we offered Chris a part-time position. Six months later, she was full-time in our finance department. During that time, Chris remained teachable. She has allowed gratitude to shift the entire atmosphere of her life and is committed to continual growth. I have watched fire ignite.

Chris has been a bright light in our office. The atmosphere of her life is entirely different today than when we met. Tears are still her currency because they come from a well of gratitude (I don't ever want that well to dry up). Ministry can be heavy, but she sets an atmosphere of appreciation. The flame in her life will increase as she allows gratitude to rule the atmosphere of her life. She doesn't miss an opportunity to thank us for allowing her to be a part of what God is doing. But honestly, we are grateful that she chooses to do the hard work every day. Chris keeps the atmosphere of her heart conducive to fire! She proved our early observations as accurate; she is one of the most intelligent people I know and was called by God to be right where she is serving today. She is an example to anyone walking through hard seasons and situations: You can adjust the atmosphere of your life if you want to! Just follow 1 Corinthians 5:17 (NLT), "This means that anyone who belongs to Christ has become a new person. The old life is gone; a new life has begun!" New life, new atmosphere.

Our prayer should be:

> God, show me the current atmosphere of my heart. Give me wisdom and grace to do what I can daily to create a place where Your fire can burn. Let Your plan be accomplished in my life. Set the atmosphere of my heart to a place that is always pleasing to You and conducive to fire.

2) Prescription

Once the atmosphere is right where it needs to be, the next thing is to determine the prescription for your heart. In a controlled burn, prescriptions target a specific need and then give the plan as a catalyst for that change. When I am sick, I walk into the doctor's office and tell the doctor precisely what is happening. He can give me exactly what I need to get better. I don't do well with trial and error or a shot in the dark. I am going into the room with a clear description of what is happening, and I want to leave the room with a clear game plan for improving. Because I have a great doctor, the game plan is executed through written prescriptions. The only way for those prescriptions to work effectively is if I follow the instructions. Now, before you judge me, let me say I usually do. But occasionally, I get a prescription I don't think I need, so I don't follow orders.

We are like this regarding God's plans if we still want control of our hearts. He has a plan for each of us. That plan comes fully equipped with mountains (victories) and valleys (trials). His plan includes different landscapes (uncharted territory), changes in direction (faith moments), and oftentimes even challenging things. We must be controlled enough to use our boundary line (tests). Our hearts cannot accomplish everything He has for our lives unless we follow His plan. Jeremiah 29:11 was a verse that sustained me when my heart wondered if God had a plan for me. In that verse, He promises that He has a plan. His plan is for our good and not our detriment. Following His plan will ensure we have hope and a future.

> *If the stronghold of control remains in your heart, you are in danger of thinking your ideas are God's ideas.*

....

I wish I could tell you that I have stuck to His plan 100 percent of the time and never gone my own way. But that would be a lie. You can relate. As hard as it is to say, I have been guilty of control issues. You may understand how that feels. But if you don't, allow me to explain. There are times that I have been following God's plan and then think He has possibly made a mistake. He placed a valley where I thought a mountain should be or a structure where I thought a turn should be. When I encountered these times, I did what any caring person would do—brought the oversight to His attention. If the stronghold of control remains in your heart, you are in danger of thinking your ideas are God's ideas.

Thankfully, God is patient. He will allow us to wander in the wilderness until we are ready to follow His prescription.

In 1999, I had this experience that lasted much longer than needed. It was the summer before my first year of college. (Yes, I graduated in 1999, and at our prom, they played Prince's "1999".... I'm confident that every school did that year.) That summer, I was completely blindsided by a relationship. Until then, I was 100 percent focused on God's plan. I knew that He had called me to Lee University, and I knew that He had called me to be in campus choir (a traveling ministry choir). I did both of those things, so in my mind, I was doing what God asked of me.

I had not planned to fall hard for someone and begin a relationship, but I did. I figured, "It must be God's plan" because everything was perfect. It remained "perfect" until I moved to college, where he had already been for two years. Only after the move did I discover that the person I had come to care for was not the one I was dating. He was a different person. Every time I broke it off, I got pulled back in. If this has ever happened to you, you understand how confusing it can be. I tried for a year and a half to make a change to follow God's plans for my life. I begged God to fix everything and make it right again. Every time, I would walk in circles. Because really, I just wanted Him to make what I wanted the right plan. I knew I had to release my will because what He had was so much better. I had been disobedient; I didn't follow His plan; I followed mine, and the consequence was pain.

I was in good company; God's very own people did the same thing in the book of Exodus, but there was a moment when I came to an altar and got honest with myself and God. During a weekly campus choir prayer meeting, I spent about an hour on my face before the Lord. I was broken, confused, hurt, and angry because God didn't hear me. He had gotten it wrong, or so I thought. God never intended to exchange His plan with mine, and I am eternally grateful. He was patient with me as I figured out how to surrender. That night,

I heard the voice of God speak inside my heart, *Melissa if you will surrender your heart, I will heal you and show you my plan.* Then I felt Him call me to a nine-month fast to draw close to Him. Every time I tell this story, I return to that moment. And my heart fills with so much gratitude.

> *While I was repenting, God was planning.*

Jesus leaves me in wonder. His Spirit is present with us! He is alive in every believer. When we mess up and turn the wrong way, He faithfully invites us back to the path. It is His will that all come to repentance. He calls our hearts to turn around and return to the right path. I am so thankful He never gave up on me. My control issues caused chaos. It took real love entering my chaos to bring healing and peace. At that moment, I experienced peace amid my self-inflicted pain. I responded to Him with a "yes" and "I surrender." Here is the coolest part. My future husband was in the same prayer meeting. While I was giving God my yes and total surrender, God was downloading a map to Justin.

What I am telling you is just as it happened. While I was repenting, God was planning and working in everything to get me to the place He had always intended. I love how intentional our heavenly Father is. It's mind-blowing. God began to deal with Justin's heart, and He heard the Lord speak to his heart, *Melissa is going to be your wife.* This information was then confirmed by another person who had no idea what God said to Justin. I can't help but see the room in my memories. I know where Justin was sitting. I know where I was kneeling. And the angle was perfect between us. Up until that moment, he and I had only been friends. But God was so intentional; over the next nine months, I fasted, and He healed. He was working out every detail.

There is wisdom that came into play. I am thankful that Justin never shared with me what God spoke until much later. Doing so might have made me run for the hills; my heart wasn't ready. Today, twenty-one years into marriage with my best friend, I can tell you that God's plans are perfect—for good and not evil. But we have to surrender to His will. The choice will always be ours, but there is only one right plan. His plan. Our marriage isn't perfect because we aren't perfect. The journey still includes mountains and valleys. But we know that God intended us for each other. Regularly, I thank God that He didn't give me "my plan" or what I thought I wanted.

God knows the right prescription to maximize the impact of the fire burning in your heart. If you surrender, the rest is easy. Just follow the plan. His track record is fail-proof. He has never failed, and He never will. He has a plan. Our job is to follow the prescription so His will can be accomplished in our hearts. When we surrender, His fire burns without restriction but with such powerful intention.

3) **Boundaries**

Once the atmosphere of our heart is conducive to fire and we follow His prescription for the plan to let the fire burn, our final step is to set up the boundaries. The fire has a specific path it is intended to follow, boundaries are set to remind professionals of the burn objective. This controlled burn in nature requires many hands and many eyes to ensure success. Our lives need others. This is about our hearts and accountability. Accountability is being held responsible for a certain standard of excellence. If the fire didn't have boundaries and expectations, no one would know when and if they were hitting the mark. Accountability is a team effort so that we can help each other hit the mark. The goal is to accomplish His plan for our life and make it to heaven.

We all need accountability. When people are held accountable, they are called to explain their behavior based on expectations. When accountability is applied correctly, it should create a positive result. In the case of a controlled burn, accountability of boundaries can mean the difference between life and death. And so it is with the heart. Accountability is for our protection. When the boundaries are clear, holding the hearts of people you care about accountable is needed. Accountability, or the lack thereof, can mean the difference between eternal life and death for another person. As believers in Christ, we need others to walk the road with us. Consistent accountability has been a path used by God to protect my heart and the hearts of those I love and lead.

Have you ever felt you needed to be protected from yourself? If you haven't, then you need accountability quickly. Accountability should be expected and welcomed in the life of a Christ follower. A sign of personal maturity is when you crave boundaries and value expectations. As a pastor, nothing blesses my heart more than seeing someone who desires genuine correction and is authentic in their desire to learn and grow. God has given me many people who love me enough to hold me accountable. I appreciate the people who have called me out in love, have approached me with grace and care, and have sharpened me to make me better. To this day, I appreciate those who have and continue to love me enough to be honest.

Everyone needs people in their lives who are permitted to say hard things. That position is earned in my life, as it should be for you. Not everyone can speak into my heart. This is a boundary you have to set. Only you know who those safe people are. The Bible gives some people that you should consider: those with spiritual authority like leaders in the church (Hebrew 13:17) and parents with authority (Ephesians 6:2). Other than those with spiritual authority, my parents, and my husband, there are only a select few I welcome in that space. I can be that for others because others love me enough to correct and hold me accountable.

There are three types of responses to accountability:
1) Those who appreciate and desire the correction
2) Those who welcome accountability but refuse correction when it is given
3) Those who don't welcome accountability and refuse correction when it is given

Which one of the three categories do you fall in? No matter which one you are in right now, you can get better. The one we should all desire is option one. Proverbs 15:32 says, "Those who disregard discipline despise themselves, but the one who heeds correction gains understanding." Wisdom partners with correction. I prefer to be corrected now than to spend eternity paying the price for my folly. A heart on fire has to have boundaries. We need accountability. We need one another to see it and say it in a way that we receive it. Value your heart and eternity enough to invite accountability. Then open your eyes and watch as growth happens. If you love correction and the desire to be disciplined, you will be counted among the wise. But if you spend your life making excuses and allowance about why you said or did the things you said or did, you will be counted as a fool. Proverbs 12:1 says, "Whoever loves discipline loves knowledge, but whoever hates correction is stupid."

We shouldn't assume that everyone understands accountability. If a person has grown up with abuse and mistrust and is surrounded by people who themselves have never been accountable, this is a new concept. Our world is full of people in this category.

It was post-COVID-19 when I met Karmella. When she and her daughter showed up at The Avenue, it felt as if we had known them all our lives. She was the joy we needed in that season. Karmella can fill a room with her voice, laughter, and personality. If you have any insecurity regarding BIG personalities, she will cause your heart to confront them. She loves big and lives big.

Karmella's whole story would take me all day to share, so I will give you the big points. She was raised in the inner city of Cleveland, Ohio. Growing up, she faced generational poverty, constant abuse, instability, family issues, and racial tensions, which led to a life bound by addictions handed to her as "normal" and "okay." Sometimes, as believers, we can be hard on people who carry addiction. I encourage you, before you judge, to listen. She is a single mom to her incredible daughter and decided she wanted more for her. Karmella moved to Tennessee to give her daughter a better life—on her own, with no family support.

Since Karmella has been at The Avenue, I have watched her throw herself into accountability. She has allowed the leaders who surround her to sharpen her personally. In just four years, she has come out of hiding. She is free from shame. She has broken addictions. She has broken generational poverty and is entirely in love with Jesus. This is what happens when fires start burning. We allow the Holy Spirit to burn what doesn't belong. We realize our issues were not as hidden as we once thought. And we surrender to His plans for our life.

When the rubber meets the road, she will be the first to tell you perfection is not her standard. But if you don't understand her journey, you cannot celebrate all her victories. Freedom has become her banner. Like all of us, she's a work in progress. She has found safety in accountability and has given herself over to discipline. She has learned for the first time that she needs boundaries. She is open, raw, and authentic. When we welcome accountability, we partner with wisdom. Hebrews 4:13 says, "Nothing in all creation is hidden from God's sight. Everything is uncovered and laid bare before His eyes to whom we must give account." So it is better to hold one another accountable in love here on earth than allow someone we say we care about to enter eternity with their sins unaddressed.

Our hearts must be set for optimal burn. We must diligently follow God's prescription to accomplish His plan for our lives. Finally, we need boundaries through accountability. Invite God into this moment and ask Him to show you if there is anything in these areas that needs to shift in your life.

ETERNAL FLAME

When the controlled fire has done its work, new life will spring forth. Things in your heart that may have been dead and lifeless will be burnt away. Promise and hope will take its place. He is faithful to renew you, restore you, and redeem you.

> *When tended to intentionally, the flame of your heart will make an eternal difference!*

We must daily tend to our flame. When tended to intentionally, the flame of your heart will make an eternal difference! The power of the Holy Spirit alive and working in us brings real change. He will burn away the landscape so dark places are exposed, and the light can allow new life to grow. The flame lit from a life securely rooted in the love of God can be maintained to accomplish the burning away of things in our hearts that used to hold us back and leave us STUCK. The old offenses will burn away. Pain from trauma can burn away. The places that felt insecure and unsafe will be burnt up. You will see yourself and others through the eyes of potential and hope. Gratitude and love will be the aroma that rises from the fire of your heart. New life will spring forth. You will see growth in areas you never imagined possible.

Tending the flame of my heart simply means that when the fire of God's love illuminates anything in the landscape of my life that needs to be removed, I allow Him to burn it away. I desire to be more like Him. When His fire comes into my heart, it changes everything for the better. Let the atmosphere of your heart attract and welcome fire. Be responsible for tending the flame, and your life can be lived with hope and divine purpose. Limitations will be removed. Anything will be possible, and everything will become clear! When this fire is burning in your heart, it should be the eternal flame; it should never go out! And because the fire stays burning, your life will be full of passion, purpose, and joy! We have to steward the flame with intentional purpose. Only then will we know our hearts beat from a place of fire!

Let the atmosphere of your heart attract and welcome fire.

Let your heart be a place where fire is always present! In that kind of atmosphere, darkness is defeated, clutter is consumed, and passion, purpose, and joy will always be present! Once you have experienced a life with the fire of the Holy Spirit, you will never want to live without Him again!

PRAYER OF COMMITMENT

Father, I invite You to make the atmosphere of my heart more like Yours. I surrender to Your plan. I commit to following Your prescription so my heart can burn. Be glorified in my life as I submit to godly wisdom and accountability. AMEN!

GUARDED TO GAIN

"Guard the good deposit that was entrusted to you—guard it with the help of the Holy Spirit who lives in us."
—2 TIMOTHY 1:14

My daughter was recently named valedictorian for her high school senior class. She has a God-given gift of intelligence. As a parent, watching her push and develop that gift has been one of the great blessings. We recognized it when she was in elementary school; she could study and understand things well beyond her years. She has always loved school. Since before she could read, books were among her favorite items. I remember her being three years old and sitting with her younger brother; she would tell a story as she flipped through the pages of a book. Her mind is a beautiful gift from God.

Like most parents, sitting at their children's high school graduation, I got lost in the memories. I remember watching her grow. She went through seasons in her education that stretched her and pushed her to her current standings. Each time she faced adversity, she put her nose to the grindstone and pushed through. She took a challenging and rigorous course load in her sophomore and junior years. Advanced placement classes and dual enrollment were two things I became very familiar with. She graduated with a year of college credits and a four-year scholarship to a private college. To say we are proud to be her parents is an understatement. My only struggle now is letting her go—she leaves for college in a few short months.

She is impressive. Not just because of what she has accomplished but because of the heart from which it flows. You will hear from her a little later in the book. (She has written an incredible reflection on the heart of a young woman.) Her mind was a gift given to her by God. The work ethic she chose to develop was her gift back to God. She has been blessed abundantly because of it. She's destined for great things with every new season. The character she possesses in her heart pushes her to gain. She has never squandered the gift and has worked for an increase.

> *If we don't stop gaining, He won't stop giving!*

I anticipate she will have the same effect on the Kingdom. She already leads and loves people deeply. She is marked to communicate to her generation in written and spoken words. She again has said yes and will spend the next season of her life gaining more wisdom and knowledge for increase. She "gets it;" increase and gain isn't just for one season of life. Instead, our lives should tell the story of gain after gain after more gain. If we don't stop gaining, He won't stop giving! He showed us this principle in Matthew 25:14-29:

> "Again, it will be like a man going on a journey, who called his servants and entrusted his wealth to them. To one, he gave five bags of gold, to another two bags, and another

one bag, each according to his ability. Then he went on his journey. The man who had received five bags of gold went at once and put his money to work and gained five bags more. So also, the one with two bags of gold gained two more. But the man who had received one bag went off, dug a hole in the ground, and hid his master's money.

After a long time, the master of those servants returned and settled accounts with them. The man who had received five bags of gold brought the other five. 'Master,' he said, 'you entrusted me with five bags of gold. See, I have gained five more.'

"His master replied, 'Well done, good and faithful servant! You have been faithful with a few things; I will put you in charge of many things. Come and share your master's happiness!'

"The man with two bags of gold also came. 'Master, you entrusted me with two bags of gold; see, I have gained two more.'

"His master replied, 'Well done, good and faithful servant! You have been faithful with a few things; I will put you in charge of many things. Come and share your master's happiness!'

"Then the man who had received one bag of gold came. 'Master,' he said, 'I knew that you are a hard man, harvesting where you have not sown and gathering where you have not scattered seed. So I was afraid and went out and hid your gold in the ground. See, here is what belongs to you.'

"His master replied, 'You wicked, lazy servant! So you knew that I harvest where I have not sown and gather where I have not scattered seed? Well then, you should have put my

> *money on deposit with the bankers so that when I returned I would have received it back with interest.*
>
> *'So take the bag of gold from him and give it to the one who has ten bags. For whoever has will be given more, and they will have an abundance. Whoever does not have, even what they have, will be taken from them.'*

Upon reading this scripture, my mind fills with so many thoughts. I am excited to unpack those thoughts with you. God created your heart for gain. Gain can only happen when we understand our assignment. The Lord has entrusted everyone with something. Gifts given by God are different for each of us. The common denominator is that we are all invited to gain for the Master. My goal is to take your heart on a journey of discovery that provokes thought, intention, and action.

THE MASTER OF YOUR HEART

Sometimes, I think about what God gave humanity, and I am completely speechless. The parable of the bags of gold was Jesus's parable about Himself—the Gift to the world—and His past, present, and future investment in us. In this parable, Christ is the Master. He is the owner of all things and people. This story shows us that He has entrusted His servants (believers) to do His work. The parable stated that He called "His servants" to Himself (v.14). The context gives us so much insight into the servants. On that day, to call a servant your own meant that the servant was born into your house, bought for a price, devoted to the master's praise, and employed to work on his behalf. And because the master had to call the servants to him, it is implied that they are busy at work. Jesus was showing the necessity of habitual preparation. This call demonstrates the need for diligence in our present work and service to the master.

> *Gain is more than just a good idea. It's an expectation.*

· ·

How can we relate to this story? It makes the responsibility of guarding our hearts so clear. Jesus lays His expectations of stewardship before us in Scripture. When we are born into the Kingdom by putting our faith in Jesus Christ, He calls us His. His blood paid the ransom for our hearts. Our hearts belong to Him. His basic expectation is that we are entirely devoted to Him as servants, working to build His Kingdom. By working in His Kingdom, we show our hearts are His. When we diligently serve him by increasing, we communicate the value we put on our hearts—the heart He paid for to live and continually grow for the glory of God and the good of others. Gain is more than just a good idea. It's an expectation.

UNDERSTANDING EXPECTATIONS

Let's clarify the word "expectation." We juggle so many responsibilities in life. With each of those responsibilities, there is a set of expectations. Expectations can be spoken, unspoken, realistic, or unrealistic. One thing I love about leading people is giving them an opportunity. Dr. Sam Chand is an incredible friend and mentor for my husband and me. He is a world-renowned leader in the secular and Christian world of leaders. The first time we had him speak to leaders at The Avenue, he shared about the three Os of leadership: observation, opinion, and opportunity. The main idea is that people are given opportunities based on the opinions that have been formed of them while being observed. That picture has never left my mind as I continue to discover and empower leaders.

Lack of clarity is one of the greatest mistakes a leader can make in empowering others. To be unclear is to be unkind. As I have grown in leadership, I have found that some of my most significant frustrations with others have been my fault. I trusted the person working for me; they were fully competent to accomplish what I needed, but I gave them an assignment without telling them the grading scale. They did not fail; I failed to express what I needed and paint them a picture. I am constantly improving, but this has happened more than I care to admit. The unexpressed expectation is premeditated frustration every time, all the time. If you don't intentionally set your expectations, someone else will set them for you; chances are you won't be happy.

I love that Christ's expectations for our hearts are clear. He never changes, nor do His expectations for us. In Scripture, He shares precisely what pleases Him. He believes in us, so He has clear expectations for us. He knows how to paint a picture. He does it throughout Scripture, but it's incredibly impactful in this particular parable. His depiction of the three servants stirs up so many emotions in me. I found myself feeling sorry for the servant over the master's rebuke. I'm envious of the one who was loaded. I was conflicted about the one in the middle. I am thoughtful about which category God might put me in if He returned today.

We all hope we will be commended. And if there is even a question in your mind, then you are in good company. We will break this down together and journey through the hearts of all three servants. But it is so important that as we do, you know this: the Master knew his servants, and the servants knew their master.

HE KNEW THEM

I shared a moment ago that the master's servants belonged to him. He had a personal investment in them. He trusted them with all he had. Gold was costly, and he handed it to each of them and walked away. He did not give out valuables haphazardly. He knew what each of them could handle, and he gave accordingly. Somewhere along the line, he saw each of their hearts and abilities. He formed an opinion of their potential according to his observations of their work and gave each of them an opportunity. The rest would be on them.

Our heavenly Father knows us. We belong to Him. He paid a debt He did not owe to buy our freedom. We are part of His royal family, coheirs to the Kingdom of God. He believes in us. That thought alone should cause you to rise higher as a steward of your life. In *The Seven Habits of Highly Effective People*, Stephen Covey said: "Treat a man as he is, and he will remain as he is. Treat a man as he can and should be, and he will become as he can and should be."[32] Christ has never treated us as less valuable when we were dead in our sins. In His mercy, He sees us, not for who we are but for who we could be. We all have a past. When we are born into the family of God through salvation, the Bible says He throws our sins as far as the east is from the west and remembers them no more (Psalm 103:12).

I desire to see myself the way God sees me. I want to see others the way God sees them. I want to be a part of pulling out the "next level" in those I lead simply because of the way I treat them. My husband and I have had the opportunity in our twenty years of ministry to meet some fantastic people. Remember the story I told you about living in Cincinnati for nine years before moving to Tennessee? In nine years of living in Cincinnati, we met and shared leadership

---

[32] Stephen Covey, *The Seven Habits of Highly Effective People: Powerful Lessons in Personal Change* (New York, NY: Free Press, 2004).

with some amazing people. (Several amazing people have moved to Tennessee since we have been here to help us lead.)

Two of the most remarkable people we met there were Todd and Jessica. We had been there for about a year when these two walked into church. The first thing we noticed was their love for people. They were people magnets. You know that type when you meet them; they always have a crowd around them. People get excited when they show up and are sad to see them leave. They bring life to any party and give a sense of belonging to others. If you don't have people like them in your life, you are missing out. I still laugh when I think about what we did, but it worked, all thanks to God!

We were young and green as grass in youth ministry. We were also passionate and needed passionate people to join us to form a youth leadership team. All it took for us was one observation, and we invited them to dinner. We had so much fun at dinner that we invited them to attend a Wednesday night youth service. After seeing them interact with the students one time, Justin and I left convinced that these two were made to work with students! All of this headed in a great direction, but we never stopped long enough to learn if they were growing in their relationship with Jesus and ready to be examples to students. In Jessica's words, "We had to pray the sinner's prayer and stop smoking all in one day; we were not about to lead those kids in the wrong way, so we knew we had to be better (lol)."

I am thankful that God sees us and knows us. Todd and Jessica were called to lead in the Kingdom! As a disclaimer, I do not encourage anyone to choose people haphazardly to lead and influence teenagers. Still, God used it to draw them back into a relationship with Him. Belonging gives people a reason to believe in themselves as Christ believes in them. God saw the heart and innocence of the young leaders we were, and He used it as an opportunity to win back the hearts of Todd and Jessica. During the remainder of our time in Ohio, they were some of our most outstanding leaders for those students. When we moved, it hurt so badly to leave them. We poured our lives out for God together in ministry; they were our friends.

For the next eight years, we only saw them a handful of times, whether they passed through or when we went back to visit family. But in 2020, they walked into The Avenue Church at the height of the pandemic. Todd is 6'5", has broad shoulders, and looks like he could take you out, so he is hard to miss. To make matters worse, he was wearing a toboggan and mask, and all you could see were his eyes. He had our security team on high alert. Todd wept for hours this day as the Holy Spirit began speaking to him about Tennessee. We didn't know they were coming. We had a wedding to perform, but we begged them to stay at our house so we could catch up. In true Todd and Jessica form, they made friends with about twenty people and went to lunch with them. They attended a hospital prayer vigil and a party before meeting with us that day!

When we finally got together at our house, we talked for hours. Catching up on life and family, they wanted every detail about The Avenue. It turns out that was the day God called them to leave everything and move down to Tennessee. Eighteen months later, in 2022, they were here for good! The blessings flowing from their lives since we first met them continue. They are passionate, competent, and full of life, love, and joy. They are the definition of compassion and servitude. Jessica even joined our pastoral staff team in 2023 as the Director of Human Resources. I am happy to report that they are still smoke-free and serving Jesus!

I tell you that story to bring to life the depth of God's connection to us. Our heavenly Father knows us. He sees our hearts. First Samuel 16:7 (NKJV) confirms, "For *the Lord does* not see as man sees; for man looks at the outward appearance, but the LORD looks at the heart." I have to believe it was the knowledge of what was inside of them twenty years ago that God saw. God knew the return from their lives would be great if they could learn to guard their hearts well. In true God fashion, He was right. He gave them Kingdom opportunity. They returned it to Him with an increase.

It makes me feel grateful like David did when he wrote his psalms of praise. Your praise is as unique as your heart. How precious are your thoughts about my heart, God? You have never given up on me. You see in me what others cannot see. Your plans for me are good. You weigh my thoughts with your mercy and see my faults through your grace! You open doors for me that no man can shut. You are a good Father!

I am so thankful He knows, sees, and invites us into MORE. He knows the potential inside of us and chooses to take a chance. The least we could do is bring Him an increase!

THEY KNEW HIM

Not only did the master know his servants, but the servants knew their master. Each of the servants was clear about the expectations of the master. They knew him well. They served Him, and they had seen him handle business. Servants in that day lived in the homes of their master, so they knew him personally. They saw his responses to his many interactions. When he was having a good day, they knew what to expect. The servants saw their master's response on the days when nothing went right, and he faced challenges.

Every time I read this, I think about our family. If you want to know who a person is, ask the people they live with. Being married for twenty-one years, I know Justin better than he knows himself. One night, while we were at home, he asked me to run out and get him something to eat. When he decided where he wanted food from,

I grabbed the keys and headed to the door. He asked me if I knew what he wanted, to which I replied, "I always know what you want anywhere I go."

When I returned, I thought seeing which of us knew the other better might be fun. I had the kids shout out a category, and we would see who had the most answers. So, if they said, "Favorite ice cream flavor?" I would say what Justin's favorite flavor (cookies and cream) was, and he would say mine (coffee). When we got the answer right, we each got a point. Justin said that the game was his worst nightmare because he felt too much pressure to answer correctly in the heat of the moment. He thought he would draw a blank and miss it because of his nerves. We played anyway because the game was fun! I bet you'll never guess who won?!?!? Yes, that's right, I won. When you live in the same house as someone else—you know a person.

We must establish that each of those servants knew their master very well. That is why the first two servants didn't need any explanation for what was expected of them. The third servant gave excuses as to why he chose not to bring the master increase. In verse 24 (emphasis added) of that passage, he says:

> *"Master, I knew you are a hard man, harvesting where you have not sown and gathering where you have not scattered seed. So I was afraid and went out and* hid your gold *in the ground. See, here is what belongs to you."*

The key words in that passage are "I knew you."

The expectations are clear regarding our faith and knowledge of Christ. He knows us, and He expects us to know Him. The only way we will ever know Him is to be intentional. He has already done what we could not; we have to put it to work for us now. He wrote His Word so we would pick it up and read it. He taught us to pray so we would pray. He showed us how to give so we would provide. He told us how important the church was to Him so that we would be a part of it. He instructed us to build a life that honors and pleases Him, so we would! For every question you have asked, He has given you an answer so you will follow Him. He told us that He was going away to prepare a place in heaven so we could be with Him forever. He told us He would come again to get us so we would be ready. What, then, will our excuse be? We have every opportunity to know Him, so we should KNOW HIM.

EVERYTHING TO GAIN AND EVERYTHING TO LOSE

The trust the master had in his servants is one of the highlights of Matthew 25. He put something valuable in their hands, and then he left. What would it take for you to hand over the contents of your bank accounts to a person and walk away? Allow me to answer the question. It would take absolute trust. These three servants had everything to lose or everything to gain. The difference was determined by thoughts (beliefs), feelings (perspective), and choices (action). (Hopefully, that looks familiar to you; if not, it might be a good time to reread chapter 2.) There is concrete evidence that the same flow applies to all of us. We must learn this because it could be the difference between life and death. Jesus is coming. He will return just as His Word tells us. What we have gained with what He has given us will be our gift to Him. I want everyone to go before Him full-handed. Let's examine the lives, decisions, and lessons the three servants wish to teach us.

A TOTAL LOSS

Trying only sometimes equals success, but not trying will always equal failure. The third servant figured this out too late. I can picture it now; the interaction with his master pre-trip was probably awkward. Even though the servant knew the master, he hadn't proven much. We know this because the master only gave each servant what they could handle. We receive from Christ in the same way that we work for Him. This concept makes a faithful and hard-working believer a magnet to favor. Faithfulness shows Christ that you honor what He gives you. Imagine what would happen if every believer became faithful and worked hard to invest in the heart they were given.

Loss for this servant didn't happen the day the master returned. It started the day He was given a talent. That is when He began losing. People do not lose everything overnight. It is a slow burn—one wrong decision after another. One heart invader left to destroy a heart. One lousy thought that turned into a belief and stole the proper perspective. One bad relationship that pulled you into the wrong place at the wrong time. We do ourselves a disservice when we do not slow down and learn from failure in our own lives and the lives of others. Failure is a great teacher. I have learned far more from my failures than my successes.

LOSS #1: HIS MIND

Your past should be the catalyst that raises your expectations of the future. Unfortunately, in the case of this servant, his mindset was negative from the start. The scripture says that he went off immediately after receiving the money, dug a hole, and hid the money. Before you think I have lost my mind, let me explain. It was the battleground lost in his mind that caused negativity. That same negative thought pattern sent him looking for a spot to dig a hole.

Have you ever been up against a challenge at work, and the thought of overcoming it felt overwhelming? Or maybe you committed to that 4:30 a.m. workout class but felt like quitting before you even started. If you are a woman and have ever been pregnant, as soon as the first muscular contraction hits, you tell yourself, *I can't do this.* All those feelings are very real. That feeling came from a thought in your mind first—a negative thought. When negativity is entertained in your heart, it breeds more negativity, leading to a downward spiral in your perspective and behavior.

The servant had done this type of work before, but his mind was given over to himself that day. Negative thoughts breed self-esteem issues and self-doubt and are destructive to self-confidence. "Self-preservation" is what the servant had on his mind; his account was overdrawn.

We can learn many things from this servant. The most important lesson here is that we must take our minds captive before they take us! Second Corinthians 10:5 tells us how: "We take captive every thought to make it obedient to Christ." That scripture means to grab your thoughts and hold them as prisoners until they agree to reflect the truth found in Christ. Don't just leave them to be destructive. Make them obey His Word. How will you know what to correct if you don't know His Word? For the servant, he knew his master's will. He knew his master's expectations, but he did not take his mind prisoner. Let's learn from this failure.

LOSS #2: HIS SIGHT

Out of sight, out of mind. The servant dug a hole in the ground and buried it. Why? It was typical in that day and time for families to bury their wealth under their homes so invaders didn't steal it. But that was not the case for this servant. The servant buried the wealth because he didn't want to deal with it. Maybe the servant thought he had plenty of time and would return to it later. Maybe he was apathetic and didn't care. Perhaps the pain of seeing it unchanged day after day was more than he could handle. If he had no intention of touching it, burying it would at least mean it would be there when he needed access.

How many times have we done this concerning our hearts? We need to address issues, but we bury them! Out of sight, out of mind. Like a child playing peek-a-boo, we put our hands over our eyes and convince ourselves that it's not there because we can't see it. If we can't see it, no one else can either. I have a saying when dealing with issues: sweep things under the rug long enough, and eventually, we will trip over them and fall flat on our faces. Henry Kissinger said, "Whatever must happen ultimately should happen immediately." This statement is an excellent way to say that if you know it needs to happen, take care of it now. It is painful to look at things that remind us of our failures; it's even worse if we don't know how to correct them.

Once a year, we visit the eye doctor to get our vision tested. I just went to the eye doctor today. She asked me, "Do you see everything clearly with your current contact prescription?" If my answer was no, she could shift things to help me see. So, I ask you, "Can you see clearly with the lens of your current perspective of your life?" If not, you may need to seek another's perspective. You could ask a friend, counselor, trusted family member, or pastor what their eyes see. If the servant had tried this, we might have told a different narrative about him today.

We all go through pain, challenges, and situations in life that we are unsure how to navigate. When uncertain, wisdom responds, "Open your eyes." Look around you and reach out for help. Others may not take away the pain of dealing with what you see, but they can show you what you can't see. They might reveal a path you've never seen before. We can try to ignore it, but an unresolved issue always comes back into our lives somehow. Don't bury it; deal with it. Your sight depends on it.

> *Excuses give fear a voice.*

LOSS #3: HIS FAITH

The servant's fearful response showed his lack of faith. Excuses give fear a voice. We already discussed the difference between excuses and explanations (chapter 1), but we know this was an excuse because the servant shifted the responsibility off himself and onto his master. That was one bold and dishonoring move. But he had lost his mind and his sight, so all wisdom was gone in his life.

If our hearts are to be guarded for gain, we must clearly understand what causes this loss. We lose our faith when we partner with fear. Notice I didn't say we lose faith when we "feel afraid." Remember our discussion about feeling versus owning. Owning fear is what destroys your faith. We've all made excuses. There is real psychology behind excuses—they are all born out of fear. Various studies have shown four primary areas of fear at the root of all excuses.

1) *Fear of Failure:* Fear of failure is when the thought of not succeeding at something paralyzes you from achieving anything great. Instead of taking a chance and possibly failing, this fear keeps us in our comfort zones. The fear of failure is ultimately the fear of shame.

2) *Fear of Judgment:* This fear causes us to protect ourselves from being judged too harshly. It can lead to various excuses, all aimed at avoiding the perceived negative judgments or criticisms of others.

3) *Fear of Change:* This fear is rooted in the need to control the outcome. Uncertainty feeds this fear, and the need for predictability and certainty fuels its rage.

4) *Low Self-Esteem:* A lack of belief in ourselves causes us to justify inaction. This fear also causes a lack of trust and belief in others.

All four of these are really about one thing: self-preservation! Self-preservation is why you make the excuses you make. It's driven by fear and intended to control one of those four fears. Faith is choked out when fear is fully grown and controlling our lives. Our excuses give voice to our fears. He didn't trust his master's intentions for him, so his faith was in short supply.

In this passage, the master ignores the servant's sad excuses and reasoning. He can see right past the servant's words and into his heart. He is super direct and calls the servant wicked and lazy! The word lazy here in this text means to shrink back, be timid, hesitate, and partner with fear. The master told the servant, you are wicked and have partnered with fear! The next move shows the catastrophic loss that occurred.

I have witnessed the invader of fear that steals eternity from people's hearts. Many years ago, we encountered a colleague in ministry whom we became close to. He and his wife had several children, and both worked outside of the home. They were the type of family who always had to "keep up with the Joneses." We were responsible to lead them. Justin and I were tasked with providing accountability to them regarding their disobedience in tithing. Accountability like this is an incredibly uncomfortable conversation, but it is needed. The issue was their disobedience, not their money. When we pointed it out to them, we discovered a sensitive spot. Finances were an area of their lives where fear wreaked havoc. Their inability to budget and live within those boundaries brought about significant debt.

Fear owned them. They couldn't be free. Bondage in your heart in one area will affect many other areas. It spreads like a virus. At the root, we would discover later, was distrust in God, problems in their home, hidden sin, and a lack of desire to change. Much like the servant in our text, this story doesn't have a happy ending. I am not sure where they are today, but it didn't take them but another year or two to leave. They had fallen out of leadership and even the church. I think about them occasionally, praying they are well and their children will grow to know Jesus. I am still left with the sadness I felt watching them surrender their lives to fear. To be honest, it was heartbreaking. We did everything we could to offer help. We offered friendship, counsel, and even accountability. Nothing we offered provided comfort, and they could no longer keep their sin hidden, so their contact with us eventually faded.

Fear's job is to paralyze you and make you lose focus. It causes you to listen to the wrong voices and reject wisdom and faith. Fear creates obstacles and keeps you from eliminating them. The worst and most dangerous effect of all is that fear makes you forget God's truth! And when a loss or refusal of truth happens, faith dies. Faith can be revived, but it takes intentional work. And in the case of this servant, he went from dead faith to eternal death.

LOSS #4: HIS ETERNITY WITH CHRIST

There is no more significant loss than the loss of our eternal hope. Losing hope is a devastating total loss. It is devastating for the servant, all who love and know him, and most importantly, the Savior who died for him. This servant was lazy. He was not eagerly awaiting His master's return. He did what was easy and convenient with no regard for consequences. He didn't think ahead and envision his master's return. He took the investment the master made in him for granted. He figured, "What's the big deal, anyway?" He needed wisdom and understanding. There was no honor for his master or the gift he was entrusted to grow. On the day the master returned, the servant was living life. He hadn't guarded his master's investment for gain. He hid it for convenience.

If this narrative sounds familiar, it is. What I just described is the world in which we live. Carrying on as if this temporary life is all there is. The world at large is giving no thought to eternity. We must show the world who Jesus is and invite them to know His love and hope. Every worship experience at The Avenue is passionate about reaching the lost. We call this drive our "why." We teach personal evangelism weekly. We put the tools and resources in our people's hands so they can confidently invite people in. On top of that, we do a big evangelistic sermon series one month out of the year. We go hard after lost souls because that is God's heartbeat.

In recent years, we did a series entitled "Rapture." And I bet you'll never guess the focus. As self-explanatory as that would seem, we learned much about the world. We sent video crews out into crowded places to ask one question. "What do you believe happens when you die?" Some of the answers we got shook all of us to the core. Some said they believe there's a heaven and hell. Other people replied, "A place of paradise." Some even said they weren't too sure. But an overwhelming number of people said, "I don't know. I've never really thought about that before." If that doesn't trouble you, you need to ask God to light your heart on fire.

Some people are so busy in this life. They have not slowed down to consider what is after death or if there is even a God in heaven who loves them. If you want an accurate dose of reality, read the book of Ecclesiastes in the Old Testament. Our lives are a vapor, and time spent only on the here and now is pointless. Everyone will be responsible for the "talent" given to them by their Savior. When He returns, He expects a return on His investment in our lives. The servant showed us He expects an increase. No excuse as to why there is none in our lives will be convincing enough. No "reason" why it was someone else's fault will be accepted. He is coming! He is coming for your heart. More than that, He is coming to collect interest and increase. The servant lost everything that day, including his soul. This should cause us to evaluate everything. The time to evaluate our hearts and the status they are in is today. When He comes, time is up!

ALL FRUIT, NO FLUFF

I am a complete sucker for happy endings. If a movie I want to see ends poorly, I won't see it. I don't care if I spoil the entire film; I must have a happy ending. While I know this is not real life, it is the narrative I want to see. Everyone living happily ever after is what I want to believe exists. Movies that incorporate animals dying or getting hurt should be completely restricted from consumption. I will be mad about it! If I pay to see a film, I need happiness—and the same is true even if it's free. Cheesy, sappy, everyone is happy type endings.

If you bring God fruit, you won't need all the fluff.

....

The best part of the story for me is when the two faithful servants come on the scene. At first glance, these two appear as the teacher's pets. If you had that same thought, it's okay. But, they don't share any thoughts or feelings. All we see of them is when they come to the master and say, "Look what we did for you." They bring an increase! Think about it this way: they don't need words; they have their own works. If you bring God fruit, you won't need all the fluff. That is what I desire. I want to take a spiritual dump truck full of the increase to heaven. If we are going to be guarded to gain, what can we learn about the lives of the two servants?

I love talking with people who get right to the point. Typically, this type of communicator is a bottom-line person: factual and action-driven. I laugh with some of my staff about how I have to edit my texts to add kindness and fluff. Small talk is great if we are chatting, but business is business. Here is the difference:

(Fluff Text): *Hey there, I hope your morning is off to a great start. (Insert happy face emoji.) Could you please give me the numbers for this weekend's services? I appreciate it. Have a great day. (Insert sunshine emoji.)*

(Fruit Text): *Hey, could I get the numbers from this weekend, please?*

I realize that some people need and prefer the fluff approach, so I do my best to accommodate them. However, people I trust have permission to be raw and straight to the point. I know their hearts, and when trust is already mutual, I can move quickly.

In this passage, the master and the servants have the same "no fluff" interaction. The servant says you gave me this, and now I am bringing you this. And the master says, "Well done; come on into heaven." No explanation is needed. Every story that Jesus tells us is intentional. He doesn't make mistakes. So, there are some things we can learn from the actions of the servants who gained and the master's response to them. Their trust was mutual, an increase happened, and the master gave eternal rewards.

GAIN #1: TRUST

> *It costs us nothing to be loved by God but everything to be trusted by Him.*

It costs us nothing to be loved by God but everything to be trusted by Him. The master, in this parable, clearly communicates the same. The servants who ended with gain were given each according to their ability. This means that on one or many occasions, the master had seen their ability to handle things. We are all wired as humans with the need for trust. The question is, can we be trusted?

The servants who produced for the master each received different talents. *Matthew Henry's Commentary* explains the meaning of giving various amounts of talent. The word "talents" means a sum of money and represents privileges and opportunities to be used in the kingdom of heaven.[33] The opportunities given to each person may be different, but the expectation of our Creator is the same. He expects us all to reach our full potential.

Whether our role in the Kingdom is "small" or "great," it is God's job to hand out the responsibility. Our role as believers is to carry out that responsibility faithfully until He returns. To do this, we must be trustworthy. Trust hinges on several vital values being active in our lives. If we, as believers, will be guarded to gain, we must possess character, competency, and a track record.

---

33 Matthew Henry, *Matthew Henry's Commentary on the Whole Bible* (Grand Rapids, MI: Zondervan, 1999).

1) **Character:** Skills can be taught, but character is the foundation. No matter what level a person rises in their giftings, it will take character to sustain a person. Traits such as integrity, honesty, faithfulness, and self-control (just to name a few) are crucial to being the recipient of another person's trust. In Proverbs 22:1, wisdom instructs us that a good name is more to be desired than the greatest of wealth. If we are going to be people in whom God trusts, we must be people of character. The character was seen in the lives of the servants.

2) **Competency:** This is a commitment to growing in knowledge. When God calls us to something, we have to do the hard work and gain an understanding of how and what to do. Prayer is obviously key. However, God gave us a brain and work ethic; how we use them determines future opportunities that are available to us. The servant who lost it all was lazy. Wisdom tells us in Proverbs 14:23 that all hard work brings profit. The question is, how hard are you willing to work to increase your competency so the gift of God in you reaches its full potential? Competency is seen in the lives of the servants, and it produces an increase.

3) **Track Record:** Talk is not enough. Suppose we are going to build trust with Christ. We cannot build confidence in our words; trust is built on follow-through and has everything to do with faithfulness and the evidence of it throughout our lives. Understanding this is simple, even for the servants. We are all trusted with different amounts because we can't all be trusted with the same amounts.

GAIN #2: INCREASE

Anything significant should be evaluated continually. How much more should we evaluate something essential to God? The only decrease to be commended in our walk with Christ is a decrease in self. The increase shows belief both in the One who called you and the assignment you've been given. Increase is the proof of a life lived in faith. Matthew 6:33 says that we are to seek FIRST His Kingdom and righteousness and all other things God will take care of. This is something the faithful servants understood in Matthew 25. They were about increasing and gaining for the master and not for themselves. Their increase for the master shows complete trust in His character. He is good, and He will reward them for their increase.

It took faith for these servants to take what they were given and see it multiply.

Hebrews 11:1, 6 (KJV, emphasis added) says, "Now faith is the *substance* of things *hoped* for, the *evidence* of things *not seen*. . . . But without faith, it is impossible to please him." These servants saw an increase because they took what their master gave them, coupled it with hope, and executed it with action. In other words, in every way, these servants were guarded to gain. Gain for the master meant gain for them as well. They knew this because they trusted the master's heart.

GAIN #3: ETERNAL REWARDS

It was a matter of life or death for these servants. When the master returned, the two servants who brought an increase were celebrated and rewarded. He even took what He had given to the wicked servant and added it to the increase of the servant with the most. What a moment of raw reflection. The master's response wasn't left up to interpretation. It was evident where he stood. There were no participation awards for the servants left with nothing. He gave one servant more than the other without regard for hurting their feelings. He will not reward them for what they have not done or what they have done halfway.

When our kids were smaller, we always loved going to watch them in their school field day events. Setting up the chairs and the tent and sitting in the scorching heat so we could cheer them to victory with two thousand other parents was always a great time. They would look for us. Glancing at the starting line to ensure we were watching made their event seem official. On our first field day, I expected the teachers to reward the first, second, and third-place winners. These were the only ribbons during my field days when I was their age. The goal is to be FIRST. To our shock, they handed ribbons to every child who raced. Every child got a ribbon, all the way from first place to sixth place. Even the children who were terrible or didn't participate at all got a ribbon. The ribbon said: "Great Job! Participation Award."

I wonder who enjoyed seeing this happen more—the child who entered every activity so they could take home a backpack littered with awards for just being present or the parent cheering their child on to mediocrity. Whichever one it was, we decided on day one that year that we would never let our children feel good about being rewarded for losing. They can bring in a ribbon if they win first, second, or third. Other than that, throw it away. When everyone is a winner, effort, hard work, and increase lose value. Before you judge us too harshly, we encouraged them to only enter the events that they were gifted in. We cheered hard and supplied the snacks. But we would never make them think that a person who gives zero effort will receive the same reward as the one who gives everything they have.

The servants understood that principle. They took what they had and gave It all, and the master was happy to reward them. God is the same way. He is going to return, and we will be rewarded appropriately. Guarding your heart here on earth will bring a better life on earth and greater reward in eternity. Not guarding your heart here on earth could cause you to miss heaven. It will be one or the other.

We have to live like we know our Master is returning. How we live matters. Who you are matters. What you and who you are connected to matters. What you allow to take root in your heart matters. Your thought life matters. Your habits matter. How you treat others matters. How you give matters. Your obedience matters. Your motives matter. YOUR HEART MATTERS. If we are going to be guarded to gain and hear the word, "Well done, my good and faithful servant," protecting our hearts is an expectation.

ABANDONED TO THE MASTER

We can see that these servants were "all in" on what they were asked to do. They didn't make excuses. There was no mistrust of the master or his request of them. We don't see them ask for clarity or offer a way for them to gain for the master while keeping some on the side for themselves. They are comfortable in their master's will because they trust the one they follow. The master asked for it, so they will make it happen. It all boils down to one thing: their hearts honored his authority.

Those two words, honor and authority, are central to the Kingdom. With any kingdom, the subjects understand that they are accountable to the king. The king's requests would be final. If the king called for you to come, you went. There was not to be the slightest hesitation or moment of reasoning because being a part of the kingdom meant serving the king. Jesus told us to seek the Kingdom first and that all the other things we need will be taken care of. To seek the kingdom of God first means I serve the King of the Kingdom only. My opinion isn't required; I am not in charge. I am a servant to the only one worthy to be the King. And I trust in His goodness. He will care for me as I care for the Kingdom. This is what honoring His authority looks like. It can never be about me; it must always be about HE—the King!

Let me stop right here! This is why Christ tells us in Matthew that the first and greatest commandment is to love Him with all our heart, soul, mind, and strength. In following that command, there is no more room to regard ourselves. Therein lies the problem with the Westernized "Christian" community. We don't get to have an opinion in the Kingdom. Follow the example of the two servants who pleased their master. Blessings and eternal increase will flow from a heart abandoned to the King. Death to self and selfishness are expectations if we will be abandoned to the King. Mark 8:35 says, "For whoever wants to save their life will lose it, but whoever loses their life for me and for the gospel will save it." When you lose your life to yourself and find your life in the Kingdom, you discover how fantastic life can be. Life will be complete and rich. You will find meaning like you have never known on the other side of selfishness.

The servant whom the master condemned was selfish. His self-focus became a fertilizer for fear and mistrust. The two servants the master commended were selfless and sold out to the king. Their abandonment to the master became a magnet for the miraculous, and they gained everything. For gain to happen, we must be abandoned to the master! Where God is regarded, feared, and honored, there will be eternal gain!

ABANDONED TO THE MISSION

I love the *Mission Impossible* movies. I like the action, suspense, effects, and trick plays that always lead to victory! Whenever the mission has been wholly introduced, the electronic invitation will always say, "This is your mission should you choose to accept it!" Then, the countdown begins for the device to self-destruct so the mission doesn't fall into the wrong hands and spoil the plans. What

I love most is that no matter the difficulty or what it requires, Ethan, the main character, always accepts. Headquarters knows this, of course, and makes him MVP for their organization.[34]

The servants who gained were like Ethan—abandoned to the mission—and both had 100 percent success. They both did everything they could with the mission they were given, and the proof was in the increase. Being abandoned to the mission is uncomplicated when you are abandoned to the master. This means your answer will always be "YES." When He asks anything of you, you say yes. You have no reservations when you have died to yourself and become hidden in your King (Colossians 3:3). If He asks you to do it, He will provide the means for the mission because you have served Him.

Being a pastor is the most humbling assignment I have ever had. It is a constant balance of leading your heart well so you can lead God's people. I will share more about that in chapter 10. We are abandoned to God, who is the Head of the church. So, even scary steps of faith somehow seem peaceful. We have learned how to rest in His peace the longer we have followed Him. But we tell God regularly that He will always have our yes. I love serving in ministry with my husband. I prefer to do all the organizing and stay beside him to assist in any way possible; that is my happy place. I can lead worship and preach when He needs me, but my favorite place to be is behind the scenes, leading our staff team. Up until July 2023, that is what God asked me to do.

After our ministry sabbatical, everything changed. I experienced a level of God's presence in my time of solitude that shifted my vision. I'm still trying to figure out what it meant. He began speaking, and I listened intently. This is what He said: *write, speak, shift.* Over the past year, I have done more writing and speaking in different settings than

---

[34] John Woo et al., *Mission Impossible* series (May 22, 1996; Hollywood, CA: Paramount Pictures).

the previous nine years combined. I have held onto the Master and accepted His mission. I've learned how to walk in faith in new ways.

The mission isn't about me. God's mission for you isn't about you. It is about the increase in the Kingdom. Serving the King can never be about what we like or feel comfortable doing in the Kingdom. Serving the King must be about doing whatever He needs or asks of us. That takes faith. Real faith has substance and evidence (increase), as we saw in Hebrews 11. We also read that without faith (substance and evidence), it is impossible to please God.

It says, "Faith is the substance of things hoped for " (NKJV). Look at that word substance. Substance. "sub" means something beneath you, while "stance" means firm or concrete, something you can stand on. When a person trusts God, he has substance beneath his feet. He's not walking around on Jell-O and on eggshells. He's walking around on spiritual steel and concrete. That is substance.

Look at it again. Faith is the substance of things hoped for. Look at the word hope—it does not imply uncertainty; it means certainty. In the Bible, hope means a divine certainty based on a sacred promise. Hope implies a certainty that is based on a word from God. Things hoped for are the things that God has promised in His Word. It is substance; it is increase. Faith is the substance of things hoped for. Not only is faith substance, but faith is also evidence. Faith is the substance of things hoped for; faith is the evidence of things not seen.

You may have heard these expressions: "What you see is what you get," or "Seeing is believing." Both of those statements are opposite of what the Bible's definition of faith is. The Bible doesn't say what you see is what you get. The Bible says: *What you don't see is what you get. With God, it's not "seeing is believing." It's "believing is seeing."* Faith is the evidence of things not seen. Friends, there is an unseen world that is very real. Hebrews 11:3 (KJV) tells us: "Through faith we understand that the worlds were framed by the word of God, so that things which are seen were not made of things which do appear." What you can see is made of things you can't see. Now we know that's true of the structure of the universe. Our universe is made of invisible atoms, a structure you cannot see. The scripture above is one of the most extraordinary scientific statements in the Bible. The things that are seen are made of those that are not seen. So, faith is the evidence of the unseen.

There is an unseen world out there. The Bible tells us in Hebrews 11:3 that the seen world was made of the unseen world. The unseen world was here first, and it will be here last. Fear wants you to feel crazy for believing in what you cannot see, but what cannot be seen is more real than what can be seen. Second Corinthians 4:18 (author paraphrase) says, "The things seen are temporary. But the unseen things are eternal."

Being abandoned to the mission means you will walk in faith. The servants who partnered with faith brought the master increase; the master turned it into supernatural gain by adding more. The master commended servants with an increase. Their faith in the master and the mission was evident by the fruit of their life. To be abandoned to the mission, you must destroy fear and excuses and walk in faith. Guarded faith is the substance and evidence you can stand on; only a life of faith brings supernatural gain! For the King is coming, and His rewards are with Him.

> *"Nothing in all creation is hidden from God's sight.*
> *Everything is uncovered and laid bare before the*
> *eyes of him to whom we must give account."*
> —HEBREWS 4:13

PRAYER OF COMMITMENT

Father, I intend to be guarded to gain. When You return, I want to offer You an increase. I want to be a faithful and trustworthy servant. May my life be abandoned entirely to You and to what You have entrusted me to do until You return. I want to live my life, so Your response to me is, "Well done, my good and faithful servant." I love You with all my heart, AMEN!

HEART RHYTHM

"Listen to advice and accept discipline, and at the end you will be counted among the wise."
—PROVERBS 19:20

A device initially created as a correction and torture device is now in the homes of around fifty-two million Americans. In 1818, a civil engineer named William Cubitt invented the treadmill. At the time of its invention, prison systems in England began using it as a "rehabilitation device." Its purpose was to cause the incarcerated to suffer and learn from their sweat. The treadmill could hold as many as twenty-four prisoners, standing side by side and separated by partitions, so they got no interaction or enjoyment from their work. The prison used the machine to do many things, such as grind corn, power laundry bins, and even store electricity (once it was invented). Four different prisons in America received the treadmill by 1822, including prisons in New York, Charleston, East Granby, and Philadelphia. By 1842, the use of treadmills had spread to nearly 60 percent of all the prisons in England, Wales, and Scotland.

By 1885, treadmills were deemed unsafe due to the number of prisoners dying from them. Most deaths were determined to be caused by heart disease or were accident-driven due to hazardous conditions.

Prisons were operating the machines ten hours a day in the summer months and seven hours a day in the winter. By 1898, treadmills were deemed inhumane and removed from all prisons by 1912.[35]

This information explains so much. I have always felt like getting on a treadmill was torture. Now, there are cold, hard facts to prove that not only are they inhumane, but they were made to torture people into submission. That is what you call sweat equity!

I have an untreated life-long issue with Attention Deficit Disorder (ADD). Let me break it down if you are unfamiliar with what that means. My mind moves a million miles an hour. I can jump to conversation topics faster than you can blink. I am, at times, easily distracted. I remember every conversation I have had with someone, but I lose my keys and phone multiple times daily. If a person talks in circles, I am likely to jump in and ask for the bottom line; emotionally, my brain cannot handle getting caught in the weeds about details that don't matter. I might start cleaning one room of my house but

---

[35] Diane Peters, "Treadmills Were Meant to Be Atonement Machines" *JSTOR DAILY*, 2 May 2024, https://daily.jstor.org/treadmills-were-meant-to-be-atonement-machines/. (Photo also found here)

walk out having only cleaned half. I will make it back and finish; it just happens unconventionally. I need change. I enjoy a challenge. I work best under pressure.

Now that you know a little more about who I am, it will not surprise you to know that I'm not too fond of treadmills. I need the outdoors to walk or at least a slight change in scenery. If I am on a treadmill, I hate to work out. If I am walking my dogs, I can work out and be in my happy place at the same time. (Sometimes, you just have to do what works for you.)

Treadmills have come a long way. They are the top-selling piece of exercise equipment in the United States. People get on treadmills for consistency and convenience. You can set a treadmill to the same speed, time, and incline each time you work out. As long as it's indoors, you can run on a treadmill no matter the weather. You can depend on the consistency of a treadmill. Oddly enough, when the doctor wants to check a patient for heart disease, they will put that patient on a treadmill and watch the activity of their heart. Treadmills do have a lot of positive uses.

The central concepts that a treadmill represents are consistency and discipline. Consistency and discipline are two characteristics that are invaluable to heart change but, at times, need to be emphasized. If anything we have shared has challenged you, that is great! Only discipline and consistency will drive success if you have identified areas that need to change. For real change to happen, it will take the partnership of consistency and the submission to discipline to see it through. Let's look at these two words and gain some insight to move us in the right direction.

CONSISTENCY IS THE KEY

"Someone who is consistent always behaves in the same way, has the same attitudes <u>toward</u> people or things, or achieves the same level of success in something."[36] A consistent person is often described as steady, reliable, even, or stable. If you are consistent, people know what to expect from you in any given situation. Consistency is an attribute that is often overlooked. Yet it is, at the core, the very nature of who God is. He is seen from beginning to end of Scripture in the person of the Holy Spirit. "Those who belong to Christ Jesus have crucified the flesh with its passions and desires. Since we live by the Spirit, let us keep in step with the Spirit" (Galatians 5:24-25). This scripture tells us that if we live consistently, we must live empowered by the Holy Spirit.

1) THE HOLY SPIRIT EMPOWERS CONSISTENCY.

Relationship with the Lord is where real change begins. The Holy Spirit is our strength, our source of boldness, and our Helper. We serve a Triune God (one God in three persons): the Father (God), the Son (Jesus), and the Holy Spirit. From the beginning until now, the Spirit has been God's consistent, never-changing presence. Hebrews 13:8 tells us that He is the same yesterday, today, and forever. We can depend on His character. If you are a believer, He is working in you.

The Spirit is alive in individuals.
- He lives in every faithful follower of Jesus (Romans 8:11).
- He exposes and convicts us of sin (John 16:7-11).
- The Holy Spirit transforms and renews us spiritually (Romans 8:9).
- He communicates God's love to us (Romans 5:5).
- He reveals Christ to us (John 15:26).
- The Spirit distinguishes the truth from a lie (1 John 4:1-3).
- He gives us a place in the church (1 Corinthians 12:13).

---

[36] *Collins English Dictionary*, s.v. "consistent," accessed June 22, 2024, https://www.collinsdictionary.com/dictionary/english/consistent.

- He gives more of His Spirit to all who ask (Luke 11:13).
- He fills us to overflow (Acts 2:4).
- He gives us power and boldness to spread the gospel and stand for truth (Acts 1:8).
- He gives vision and prophecy (Acts 2:17-18).
- He develops God's character traits in us (Galatians 5:22-23).
- He frees us from the power of sin (Romans 8:2).
- He gives direction, comfort, and encouragement (John 14:17-18, 26-27).
- He helps us pray (Romans 8:26).

If we are to have the character of God, then we will need to be consistent. We know the nature of the Spirit of God is consistent. To *keep in step* with the Spirit, we must learn to be the same throughout our lives so that the Spirit's power can flow freely. He wants to use every person for the glory of God on earth!! The Spirit is the daily sustaining, inspiring, and guiding power of the Christian's life. He is the domain of power and sphere of influence which replaces *the flesh* as the energy force of our lives. He is the One who will help us to guard our hearts daily. If you try to live without Him, it's only a matter of time before you get tripped up.

2) CONSISTENCY MUST BECOME A HEART RHYTHM.

Craig Groeschel, leader and pastor of Life Church, says, "Successful people do consistently what other people do occasionally."[37] I believe that statement with every fiber of my being. A routine or schedule must be practiced for new habits to stick. Before they stick, we will likely have days where we fail. What is essential in practice is that we improve. We don't stop practicing because of one bad day. You can do this, just be consistent and watch your life change.

---

37 Craig Groeschel, X post, November 21, 2019, 6:00 am, https://x.com/craiggroeschel/status/1197469720775184385.

My husband is consistent in every area of his life. I like to tease him because he is so regimented in his routine. If I try to change it, it can ruin his whole day. He gets ready in the same order each day. From his shower to getting in his car, he has the process down to a science. Because of this, he is never late. He knows how to brush each side of his mouth. He counts the swipes of deodorant. He has a specific order in which he puts on his clothes, fixes his hair, and even sprays his cologne on the same spots every day. I am fascinated by his consistent routine.

If you are starting to feel a little anxious because that is not your personality, let me encourage you to breathe. You can be consistent without being rigid. I am consistent about what items I need to do to get ready. Justin has a military rhythm about his consistency, and mine looks more like a free-range chicken. Both are effective; what matters is that the core practice is there. I keep the routine interesting.

3) CONSISTENCY IS A MATTER OF THE HEART.

Personal conviction and belief must drive any area of our life that needs to change. If something is not personal, then it's not sustainable. For example, pool workouts are great and will help you achieve your desired results, but if you prefer to avoid the pool, it wouldn't make sense to get a pool membership. You would never go. Just because something works for me doesn't mean it will work for you. You have to know you want the change. Believe that the cost of consistency is worth it. Know that you can change and make a plan to get there. Consistency is not easy, but anything worth having comes at a high cost. You will need your heart to tell your head on some days why you will not quit.

One of the most rewarding experiences for me is hearing about someone's life transformation. When you lead people, you see the pain they carry. You also witness their joys, and that helps you get through sadness. Wendi is a close friend of mine. I met her many years ago, but it wasn't until 2019 that I got to know her. It's wild how you can meet people and click like you've known each other all your life. Hers is a friendship authentically forged with genuine and raw conversations. She amazes me! This woman has home-schooled all four of her children. She leads life groups for teenagers and married couples. Wendi earned her master's in counseling just a few years ago and works as a counselor. She puts Paula Dean to shame in the kitchen and loves serving people. On top of all of that, she is a fantastic friend. When we spend time together, hours of conversation and laughter feel like minutes. Everyone needs a Wendi in their life.

Wendi has worked hard to overcome the pain and devastation that life brought her through no fault of her own. She made decisions to do what was best when it was challenging. Wendi has sacrificed in silence. She showed up when she didn't have to, even when staying in bed would have been easier. She has walked through seasons of betrayal on all fronts of life and has done so with grace. She chose to get up daily, face challenges and pain, and never lose her joy. Tears were currency for her consistency, but her life today proves the process of consistency worked. She loves Jesus with all she has and is changing many lives. Wendi stayed consistent in showing up, working hard, and persevering in the good and the bad times. Her consistency was a matter of the heart. Consistency healed her heart. Staying consistent, no matter what comes your way, changes you and the world around you. We must have the Holy Spirit to empower us. When we practice consistency that comes from the values in our hearts, our lives will change for the better.

4) DISCIPLINE IS NOT A BAD WORD.

Discipline is simply this: doing what you need to do so that you can do what you want. I have had many jobs in the last twenty-five years, some that I loved and some that I endured. No matter their category, they were all beneficial for me. What does a disciplined person look like? *Merriam-Webster's* definition of "discipline" (to describe a person) is: "marked by or possessing discipline; self-control, orderly or prescribed conduct or pattern of behavior."[38] Disciplined people follow a standard set of behaviors that allows them to be self-controlled. If this crucial behavior is absent in your life, guarding your heart will be impossible. Discipline pulls the door of your heart closed and can hold fast when all other defense systems fail.

5) THE HOLY SPIRIT PROVIDES DISCIPLINE.

I love Hebrews 12:11: "No discipline seems pleasant at the time, but painful. Later on, however, it produces a harvest of righteousness and peace for those who have been trained by it." In this verse, I hear wisdom's call to accept the pain of discipline to have a life of purpose. We must have the Holy Spirit to assist us as believers because discipline denies what my flesh desires. Holy Spirit-empowered self-denial pleases the Lord and brings eternal life. The Holy Spirit is an extra layer of accountability in my heart. He points out what needs to be corrected and gives me the strength to see it through.

6) DISCIPLINE CORRECTS THE HEART.

Discipline does what needs to be done, even when you don't want to. Self-discipline shows God that you are trustworthy. When you lead your life well, you can then help others. People always tell me they want to do something BIG for God. I am their loudest cheerleader in that pursuit. However, if a heart is not stewarded

---

[38] "*Merriam-Webster Dictionary Online*, s.v. "discipline," accessed June 22, 2024, https://www.merriam-webster.com/dictionary/disciplined.

well, it will have little traction in the lives of others. A story I read recently in 1 Samuel 2-5 has been turning in my heart and mind for months.

In the story, a man named Eli is a priest for the people of Israel. He has two sons named Phinehas and Hophni. The Bible clearly tells us that Eli's sons were wicked. They stole the choice meat from the people who came offering sacrifices to God. Both men slept with prostitutes at the temple gate with no remorse. God says their hearts were wicked. All the people saw their wickedness. Imagine the church hurt they caused. For whatever reason, Eli asks his sons why they are sinning against God, and he tells them what they are doing isn't okay. Eli's response infuriated God, sending a messenger and Samuel the same message about Eli and his family line. God was angry because Eli had chosen his sons over his devotion to God. In 1 Samuel 3:12-13 (NLT), God says this to Samuel: "I am going to carry out all my threats against Eli and his family, from beginning to end. I have warned him that judgment is coming upon his family forever because his sons are blaspheming God, and he hasn't disciplined them."

Wow! God wasn't playing. You may think, "Wait, Samuel did discipline them!" He went to them and confronted it. It would be like finding one of my children stealing cars in the church parking lot and then saying, "Everyone knows what you have been doing; people are talking. You should not be stealing cars out of the church parking lot. It is not okay." All I have done is point out his wrongdoing. That is not discipline. It is observation. Anyone with eyes can do that!

What Eli did made God angry. Eli chose to regard his sons before God. In fact, through the prophet, God asked Eli, "Why do you give your sons more honor than you give me?" God tells him no one in his family line will live to see old age; in fact, both of his sons were going to die on the same day. Fast-forward to the end of the story. Both of his sons go to battle with Israel to fight the Philistines. The ark of the covenant is stolen, and both of his sons die. When the messenger comes back to Eli to report this tragedy, Eli falls off his stool, breaks his neck, and dies.

> *You cannot point out what has to be pulled out.*

If I have ever been shown the revelation of God through Scripture, this was one of those days. There are so many things at work here. But the Lord showed that you cannot point out what has to be pulled out. In other words, pointing out their sin was pointless without requiring repentance and change. Sadly, I fear so many believers today fall into that same trap. Pointing things out is easy; eyes are all that is necessary, but pulling things out is hard work. It takes proper discipline. It means that you run the risk of upsetting people. It can make us uncomfortable.

We might think acknowledging something is the same as action, but we would be mistaken. If we want hearts that please the Lord, we must recognize the issue and take steps to see change. Eli didn't do this for his sons. He was the only one who could, and he failed. When we know how the story ended, everything becomes clear. First Samuel 4:18 (NLT) says, "When the messenger mentioned what had happened to the ark of God, Eli fell backward from his seat beside the gate. He broke his neck and died, for he was old and overweight."

> *You cannot pull out of others what is rooted in YOU.*

He fell off his chair, broke his neck, and died because of gluttony. He couldn't pull out the sins of his sons because he was living in his own sin. An epidemic among believers is that we don't discipline our hearts, so we cannot require those around us to discipline theirs. An undisciplined life is a gluttonous life, extending far beyond being overweight. Gluttony slows you down. It creates baggage and heartache. You cannot pull out of others what is rooted in YOU.

Perhaps the most heartbreaking detail of all is that the lack of discipline caused the presence of God to be taken from their entire nation. The Philistines stole the ark of the covenant, where God's presence had dwelt among them. It was gone. The news headline would read: "30,000 men were killed, our priest and his entire family destroyed, and the presence of God has gone missing." All because of poor stewardship.

Hear the cry of God between the lines of this story as He begs for the hearts of His people: *Live for Me. Love Me first. Correct the things that have gotten into your heart and caused chaos. Repent from your sin and turn back to Me. I want to dwell among you. But where sin is welcomed and entertained, I cannot remain.* He is the same God, and neither He nor His words change. That is the same invitation He gives to us today. Choose discipline, choose correction. In them is life.

7) DISCIPLINE PROTECTS THE HEART.

A life surrendered to Jesus understands that following Christ's expectations protects us. There is safety in living a life that is humbly laid open and bare before the Creator. Belief is how we *say* we surrender our hearts to God. Discipline is how we *show* that our hearts are surrendered. There is protection in living a life of discipline. When our hearts are surrendered in that way, our future is secure, and in that security comes the joy of living in His promises.

Recently, we had tornados in our areas. This is rare for this part of Tennessee, but it happened. We were under a tornado watch all day because the conditions weren't favorable. When the sirens on my phone went off as a warning, and the news stated a tornado was a couple of miles away from our home, we stopped everything. We went to the basement and waited out the storm. We were protected because we took action and did what was best. We had other things to do; it caused an interruption in our schedules, but at least we were safe. There is wisdom and safety in obeying those who know more than you about the weather. They are tracking the storm, and they see what you cannot. We have the easy part, which is to act.

There is no difference in our response to Christ. When the sirens go off, we are instructed on what to do. We have to discipline our hearts to do what He says to do. In those moments, it is not wise to question, reason, or justify a different plan. Discipline does the right thing no matter how difficult. No matter the inconvenience, we trust He sees so much further down the road. His radar detection system is foolproof. Discipline takes us to a place of safety. Our hearts can settle and find rest in knowing He controls the outcome. Obedience to His Word is critical! We need to allow the Holy Spirit to discipline us. Let discipline correct our hearts and rest in the protection that discipline brings our lives.

CLOSE YOUR RINGS

Part of discipline and consistency is finding a way to track your progress. I love my Apple watch. It helps me because it gives me a visual of my progress and what I still need to do to hit my goal. It makes me want to compete against myself to beat the clock and close all my rings. The only downside is the shame you feel when you have yet to promptly accomplish what you set out to do. The friend inside your Apple watch will send you messages like, "What in the world are you doing with your life? Get up and move already!" or, "There's no way you'll finish this today; maybe you should settle for just one closed ring." (Okay, it doesn't say that, but that's what I hear because that is my lens!)

The significant part about the three rings of an Apple watch is they are a great way to see how consistent and disciplined you have been. You can see your progress by day, week, month, and year. The watch also gives you awards and badges for completing tasks. You can add an accountability partner to help you stay motivated. And it has a million workout resources and ideas to plug into the calorie counter. Reorganizing, mapping the journey, and creating a plan is where it all begins. Let's discuss creating a plan to close each of our "heart rings." Just like the watch, let's break down the three areas we need to create a plan so that with consistency and discipline, we execute that plan. The three heart rings are: *spiritual, mental (emotional), and physical.* Leaving any of these areas unaddressed will affect ALL of them. Just remember, life is a marathon. How do you win a marathon? The answer is simple: one step at a time.

GET YOUR STEPS IN

I need a clear and straightforward plan. We will use the same process to help us create the best strategy to close all the rings. After all, our minds, bodies, and spirits are well worth it! So, let's begin to break this down.

START WITH "WHY"

What is my goal? You must define the goal for anything to know when you've achieved it. Your goal is the result. "I will read through the entire Bible in a year," "I will stop drinking," or "I will forgive my father."

How am I going to achieve this goal? Success will require breaking down your goal into simple, clear, manageable steps. I encourage you to start small; some must begin with hourly or daily goals. Most can follow a daily checklist of goals. But charting the goals daily, weekly, and monthly will help your mind to compartmentalize. Write them down or type them in your notes. For example:

- The **What**: *"I will read through the entire Bible in a year."*
- The **How**:
  » Daily: *"I will find an plan on YouVersion that I can stick to."*
  » Daily: *"I will make time every morning at 6 a.m. to sit down and read."*
  » Weekly: *"I will keep myself accountable with a friend."*
  » Monthly: *"I will plan a day to 'make up' any days I miss."*

Doing things this way gives you clarity. It defines the path you need to walk on your journey. Benjamin Franklin said, "If you fail to plan, your planning will fail," and he is right. Every dream or desire of the heart must have a plan to accomplish it. It is actually fun to create.

Yield to the Process. Celebrate small victories. Be realistic but challenge yourself at the same time. Set yourself up for success by thinking and planning. Failing one day doesn't mean you have failed. The good thing about the journey is that He gives us tomorrow. When you fail, get back up, pick up your plan, and start again.

No matter what happens, keep moving. Whenever I tried to create a healthy life habit, I encountered trials and things that made me want to quit. Don't quit. Stay consistent, stay disciplined, and watch what happens as a result. Let's go! It's time to break the three areas (spirit, mind, and body) down so we know God's expectations for them; otherwise, we cannot set our own goals. He has a standard for us and goals He wants us to strive for. He wants to see us win the race in spirit, mind, and body.

SPIRITUAL RING

This ring must be addressed first. Our walk with Christ must be the foundation. If this piece is off, all the others will be out of line. I want to ensure everyone understands that salvation is the absolute first step. If you aren't in a relationship with Him, nothing I have shared with you in our time together will matter. Salvation is just the first step. There is a depth in the Spirit of God available to anyone who wants more of Him. I am NOT telling you that you need to work or try harder. I am telling you to stop all the doing and start focusing on being! Learn how to be with Jesus.

> *If we don't know His Word, we don't know Him.*

When you follow Jesus, surrendering to His Spirit is not an option. It's an expectation. If I am going to win the war over my flesh, then I must surrender. When I am in a state of surrender, I am not moving; my job is only to listen and follow instructions and move when I am told to move. The Holy Spirit wants depth in our lives, but first, we must die to self and sin. Then, choose to step with the Spirit. This is a daily choice, but it is also a choice we all have to make.

Being in step with Him spiritually means making prayer, worship, and the Word the anchors in our lives. When Christians struggle spiritually, it is because we are **Word-deficient and Spirit-deprived**. We aren't experiencing the fullness of a relationship with Him because we don't know His Word. If we don't know His Word, we don't know Him. This causes people every day to misquote Him. Our belief is founded on sand if we claim a promise He never made. We cannot bring the Holy Word of God to our level to try and justify our faith and actions. Just because you don't feel wrong doesn't make it okay. He is God, and His Word stands forever. We tread on dangerous ground if we miss this truth. If it's not found in the Word, it's not from the Lord. We are not God; God is in charge. We can't understand God's ways because we aren't Him. We get to yield to Him and receive the joy of a heart hidden in Christ. It is with this understanding that we must approach our goals and expectations. You can add to this list as you see fit, but I want to give you some foundational truths about where you can begin:

CONSISTENT HABIT TO START:	DISCIPLINE TO DO IT:
Reading Your Bible Daily: So you can know God, know His character, understand His expectations, and experience His promises.	Buy a Bible translation that helps you understand Scripture. Find a good Bible commentary to use. Choose a plan to stick to. Make time every day to read or listen to His Word. Utilize free resources: YouVersion App (Bible plans)

CONSISTENT HABIT TO START:	DISCIPLINE TO DO IT:
Establishing a Routine of Prayer: Prayer is two-way communication. There are times to speak and times to learn and listen in quiet solitude.	Read Matthew 6:9-13. Understand you pray to the Father in the name of Jesus. Pray continually—acknowledge and invite God's presence throughout your life. Listen for Him to speak, sit, or walk in quiet solitude and listen.
Connect to a Life-Giving Church: Understand that Christ died for the Church. He believes in the global church, and so should we. You were designed to need others for growth and accountability. As believers, we are stronger together and should be reaching others for Christ, making disciples.	Ask a friend for suggestions. Know what they believe, making sure you are connected to sound teaching. (ALL BIBLE) Find a place where you belong and can connect. Attend, serve, and give faithfully.

Remember, it's just the beginning. Set a rhythm, create consistent habits, and discipline yourself to see them through in this area first. We are busy with life's demands, schedules, kids, work, and church, so surrender has to be a daily choice. Life never stops. Your walk with Christ must be intentional. The Spirit wants to use you in every season of your life! Learn how to spend more time with God and you will always be in step with the Spirit. Closing this ring isn't about perfection. It's about being sensitive to Him! The Spirit makes it easy to love and serve God. We must close this ring.

EMOTIONAL RING

Emotional inconsistency is one of the biggest challenges to your growth in God and being in step with the Spirit. Let me tell you, your emotions—although very real—cannot be trusted. If you want to get your steps in your mind, you must be surrendered to the Holy Spirit. Some emotions and thoughts can't stay if we are going to get in step with the Spirit. We can't use the words "that's just the way I feel" to excuse wrong emotions. We must allow God to speak to us about how He wants us to be. Remember what we read earlier: emotions come from a group of interconnected structures deep within the brain. It's the part of the brain responsible for behavioral and emotional responses. THINK, FEEL, ACT. You need to feel things and learn how to process thoughts and emotions through the Word of God. You shouldn't be an emotional stuffer! It would be best to invite the Holy Spirit into that part of your life to lead your emotions.

That's why the Word repeatedly tells us to renew our minds and take captive every thought, bringing it under submission (2 Corinthians 10:5). We take captive every thought to make it obedient to Christ. When we don't get in step with the Spirit of God, our emotions will rule our lives. When your life is ruled by your emotions, you will always be unstable.

You have to get in step with the Spirit and take whatever emotion you are feeling, hold it, apply the Word, and then make sure you have the proper perspective. He gives us a road map if we don't know how to process emotions. James 1:5–8 says:

> *If any of you lacks wisdom, you should ask God, who gives generously to all without finding fault, and it will be given to you. But when you ask, you must believe and not doubt, because the one who doubts is like a wave of the sea, blown and tossed by the wind. That person should not expect to receive anything from the Lord. Such a person is double-minded and unstable in all they do.*

Feel what you need to feel, but don't allow those emotions to take over your life. Surrender them to the Spirit of God and respond to His leading so He can shift your perspective. We wrestle not against flesh and blood but against principalities and powers of the air (Ephesians 6:12). We do live in the flesh. If you don't stop your thoughts and make them surrender to the Spirit, you will lose every battle—especially to social media which has become the enemy's favorite place to mess with your head! The person behind that keyboard is not your enemy; the enemy uses them as puppets. Feel however you need to feel, process it through the Word, and act accordingly! Consistency in your thoughts and emotions will change your vocabulary, actions, and choices. No matter your season, your life becomes more intentional and dependable when you add consistency.

If you are emotionally exhausted from trying to do it all, I invite you to breathe in the presence of God. Ask the Holy Spirit to help you rest in Him and BE with Jesus. Stop trying to control. Stop trying to have all the answers. Just relax in His sweet presence and let peace be in the center of your mind. Here are some habits you can begin:

CONSISTENT HABIT TO START:	DISCIPLINE TO DO IT:
Start by Searching: Ask God to search your heart and your mind. Invite Him to show you where unhealthy thoughts and perspectives may be hiding.	Get a journal: Write your prayers and thoughts about what God shows you. Consider doing a topical study on what God highlights for you. If needed, contact a trusted friend to share and process your thoughts. Choose someone who is spiritually mature.

CONSISTENT HABIT TO START:	DISCIPLINE TO DO IT:
Evaluate Relationships: Look at the relationships in your life. Are you surrounding yourself with emotionally healthy people? (Pay special attention to those in your inner circle.)	Make changes. You become who you are connected to, so choose your friends according to who you want to be and where you want to go. Be honest with people and share if things are bothering you. It will sharpen you both.
Develop Emotional Maturity: Ask God for wisdom and the courage to grow. Invest in your development.	Consider seeking education on emotional intelligence (knowing yourself) and emotional regulation (recognizing and controlling unhealthy emotions). Deep dive into God's Word and ask Him for guidance.

The key to success is consistency and discipline. As you run your race, celebrate the wins and learn from the losses. God is with you, He sees you, and He is so proud! You are growing closer or further away from God, one thought at a time! We must stay committed to closing this ring.

PHYSICAL RING

Elisabeth Elliot once said, "Discipline, for the Christian, begins with the body. We have only one. It is this body that is the primary material given to us for sacrifice. We cannot give our hearts to God and keep our bodies for ourselves."[39] What a powerful thought that is, indeed. In all my days of ministry life, this is a topic that makes the most people uncomfortable. Trust me, at times, it is hard for me

---

[39] Elisabeth Elliot, *Discipline: The Glad Surrender* (Ada, MI: Revell, 1985).

to hear, too, but what in God's Word hasn't cut us at some point? First Corinthians 6:19-20 (NLT) tells us:

Don't you realize that your body is the temple of the Holy Spirit, who lives in you and was given to you by God? You do not belong to yourself, for God bought you with a high price. So you must honor God with your body.

This shell that houses your mind and soul is a temple. Once Christ died and was resurrected, the veil was torn in the Old Testament temple, and the Holy Spirit came to dwell in the hearts of all who receive Him. What an incredibly powerful truth. That means, according to this scripture, our bodies and the rights thereof belong in the hands of our Creator. Since our bodies are temples, let's think about them as the church building:

- My body is a place set apart for holiness and worship.
- My body should be kept and treated with honor.
- When people come into my life, their lives should be changed.
- I was created to connect with others.
- My body is a place where heaven touches earth.

There is no other way to see the scripture. It is His body, not yours. It is not your choice. I have read every Bible commentary I can find and have searched for any other meaning. All roads lead back to one. This is more than an idea. It is an expectation. Now, we ask God for the strength to do what is needed to make necessary changes so that He is glorified through this temple. This is when you may think about putting the book down because it's hard to hear. This is what I know about you: you can do hard things. You want the truth; that is why you've reached this point.

I believe in you. You are not alone. The Holy Spirit will breathe on you with the strength you need to accomplish the task. There is no better time than the present. You can start right now. Ask Him to search you and show you what in the temple of your life is not the way He wants it. Be brave enough to listen and respond. Remember, one day at a time, one change at a time; He is worth it. I have openly shared the change in my life, and that is what I pray for you! He is still working on me, I have yet to arrive. Each new day, I grow to love what He is doing more and more. Here are some habits you could start immediately:

CONSISTENT HABIT TO START:	DISCIPLINE TO DO IT:
Start by Searching. Invite God to show you what about your temple doesn't please Him, and be brave enough to respond when He does.	Get a journal: Write your prayers and thoughts about what God shows you. Consider doing a topical study on what God highlights. If needed, reach out to a trusted friend to share and process your thoughts, and choose someone spiritually mature.
Evaluate Your Health: Look at practical things, well visits, bloodwork, vitamin levels, etc. Make changes, so God is glorified in you.	Educate yourself about what your body needs. And give your temple the gift of health. Repent for not taking care of yourself, then set new healthy habits and stick to them.
Develop Temple Mindset: Ask God for wisdom and the courage to grow. Invest in your development.	Are there behaviors you are participating in that misuse the body God gave you? Are there relationships that need better boundaries? Have you bought into the lie Satan is selling the world, that you can live in ways opposite of a temple?

The key to success is consistency and discipline. As you run your race, celebrate the wins and learn from the losses. God is with you, He sees you, and He is so proud! You are growing closer or further away from God, one step at a time. You will close this ring every day!

PRAYER OF COMMITMENT

Father, Your Word challenges me, and it is so good. Help me see myself the way You see me. Please show me the areas where discipline and consistency need to shift in my life. Give me grace on this journey and healing when I need it. I am committed to making sure my life honors You. AMEN.

SHAME-FREE ZONE

"Therefore, if anyone is in Christ, the new creation has come: The old has gone, the new is here!"
—2 CORINTHIANS 5:17

Don't follow your heart; the heart is deceptive above all things (Jeremiah 17:9). Lead your heart to understand whom it belongs to—your Creator. You must lead your heart hidden inside the Lordship of Jesus Christ, your Creator. He created your heart with a purpose. Your heart is unique from anyone else on planet Earth, made with the intention of God, who intends to use it for His glory. The thought of how personal our God is to each of us is overwhelming. He wants to be the One we love and long for in the core of our hearts. He desires that we delve into a relationship with Him that is deep and meaningful.

The world around us is running, questioning, searching, and longing for purpose. There is a longing in the heart of every person to connect with their Creator. Sometimes, it feels unclear why you are lost, but you know something is missing. To live without Christ is like living as an orphan, anchorless without a place to derive meaning and purpose. True fulfillment and purpose become apparent when you know God. All of a sudden, everything makes sense. Hope and purpose light up your heart like a fire on a cold night. Joy and restoration course through your veins, reviving dreams you didn't know existed. And with every beat of your heart, you can feel Him drawing you closer. No one has to tell you He loves you; when you finally experience Him, you feel it. His love awakens every emotion and invites us to live in a way we never knew was possible.

Why would God go to all that difficulty for each of us? He knows everything we've done. Why would He want us, much less choose us? You may have had similar thoughts; I know I have. Here is what I have discovered through my relationship with Him and His Word: He is our Father, has an eternal investment in us, has a unique purpose for us, and wants to spend eternity with us. Each of those reasons could stand alone. All of them together speak to a love so overwhelming and intentional we could never fully comprehend them in our human minds. Those reasons are enough for me to surrender my heart to Him forever. When I surrender, He fills me with the Holy Spirit, and the Holy Spirit becomes the outflow of my heart.

JESUS DEFEATED SHAME

Shame creates a toxic atmosphere in a person's life. Everyone experiences shame, but you cannot allow it to rule you. In other words, recognize when you feel it, but don't own it. *Psychology Today* had this to say regarding shame:

> *Shame involves negatively judging yourself when you believe you've failed to live up to your standards or the standards of others. Shame evokes intense discomfort and sometimes a desire to hide; people may feel worthless, stupid, foolish, inadequate, or "less than." Shame can paralyze people, forming the lens for all self-evaluation.*[40]

---

[40] "Shame," *Psychology Today*, accessed June 24, 2024, https://www.psychologytoday.com/us/basics/shame#:~:text=A%20consistent%20sense%20of%20shame,anger%2C%20depression%2C%20and%20anxiety.

Nothing is so detrimental to a believer's heart than allowing shame to plant roots in your heart. Shame causes you to hide, taking you right back to what Adam and Eve did in the Garden of Eden after sinning (Genesis 3:8). They were unsuccessful then. We are not successful at hiding now. God knew shame would have to be defeated because it is a byproduct of sin and misuse of the heart. That's why the Father sent Jesus to be crucified! When Jesus took our sins and shame upon Himself, He broke the power of shame once and for all. He paid the price for our freedom.

> *The Holy Spirit cannot overflow from a heart bound by shame.*

The apostle Paul wrote the entire book of Romans as a letter to explain the grace and love of God. That love brought back our hearts through Jesus's sacrifice on the cross. Paul addresses shame in Romans 5. He tells us that we have been made right because of our faith in the grace of the complete work of the cross. Then he tells us that all we have been through or will ever go through is to bring glory to God through hope. That hope refers to the death and resurrection of Jesus. He admonishes against shame in Romans 5:5: "And hope does not put us to shame, because God's love has been poured out into our hearts through the Holy Spirit, who has been given to us." It's His love poured into our hearts when we come into a relationship with Him that breaks shame.

If Jesus defeated shame and told us His Spirit broke it the day we confessed Him as Lord, who are we to try and keep it alive? When we own shame, we cheapen the sacrifice of the cross. When we live in shame as believers, it silences the Holy Spirit. The Holy Spirit cannot overflow from a heart bound by shame. When we know Christ, we are all forgiven of our sins and guilt. No matter how great or small, our job after salvation is to ensure our hearts remain a shame-free zone.

If watching God redeem hurting and broken people excites you, you would love Melissa's story. Melissa was raised by a single mother who took her to church every Sunday. She was saved at thirteen but got involved with friendships that pulled her away from God and the church. Her friendships brought her to a place she never thought she would go. Smoking weed for "fun" turned into cocaine use, which led to crack. By the age of twenty, she was a full-blown drug user. At her lowest point, she moved out of her mother's home and into a crack house with her boyfriend. For twelve years, she was on a vicious cycle of addiction and abuse. There were seasons she would get clean and sober; in those seasons, she gave birth to two babies. Self-sabotage plagued her sobriety, and she would end up in the cycle of addiction again. Some years felt like days because of the drug haze she lived in, but she remembers the day everything changed.

While on a drug binge, lying on a mattress alone and hopeless, she heard the Holy Spirit's voice in her heart; it was the same voice she knew as a child. He called her out of where she was, told her to get up, get clean, and leave that life so she could raise her daughters. That is just what she did. In 2017, the same pull that called her out of addiction brought her into our lives. She rededicated her life to Christ, and she has never looked back. Fast-forward to today, she cares for people in a way I could not. She has beautifully reached people's hearts because of her unique perspective and life experiences. I have witnessed her transformation with my own eyes; she walks in victory. I get the privilege of watching her in action daily as she serves people. Her love is deep. Her compassion is rare, and her shame is defeated. She is alive in her purpose. No one has to remind her how far Christ reached out to rescue her soul. She lives every day and is indebted to His gift. Her compassion and care for others is stunning to behold. I am thankful that she has chosen to allow the Holy Spirit to flow out of her freely. Her heart has evicted shame. She draws from a well of freedom!

SHAME IS DEFEATED.... SO LIVE IN FREEDOM!

Like the story you read, we are all called to allow the Holy Spirit to flow through us to others. He wants to use your heart. Your unique perspective, history, and personality are to bring Him glory. Here are the ways to ensure life flows freely—from God, through us, and to others: *posture your heart, receive the rain, and open the floodgates.*

POSTURE YOUR HEART

> *"He says, 'Be still, and know that I am God; I will be exalted among the nations, I will be exalted in the earth.'"*
> —PSALM 46:10

This scripture is powerful. Those words "be still" do not mean "stop." In this text, the words mean "to move to a lower level." What a powerful thought. Move to a lower level, so Christ can be seated above you. In John 12:32, Jesus said, "And I, when I am lifted up from the earth, will draw all people to myself."

When we posture our hearts from a lower level, Jesus uses our hearts to draw all people to Himself. God is glorified on the Earth through your story and my story! Every believer's life has a purpose: to be lived for the glory of God! Other people are changed when a life is lived for the glory of God.

No one can tell the story of what God has done in your life better than YOU.

Christ set us free so that we could live in His freedom. It is not hard to understand and live in this freedom when my heart is postured where it belongs. A heart postured for His glory doesn't try to draw strength from its own "goodness;" we know He alone is good. We never have to worry about being enough because we recognize we aren't—only He is enough. We don't accept shame and live in it. I postured my heart in the correct position, and the only thing in my line of vision was His grace and mercy. Those are thoughts of complete freedom. Acts 17:28 says, "For in Him we live and move and have our being." We are His kids; He will never let us down when we live in that place.

No matter what I have done, where I have been, or who has influenced my heart in the past, I am free because I am in Him. This brings 2 Corinthians 5:17 alive—our hearts are postured under Christ, and living in Him means the old has passed away, and the new has come! I have so much joy when I move my heart to a lower level. With my heart hidden in Christ, He gives me a new life. A life lived in this place is free. God gets all the glory when people see and hear the sound of freedom flowing from me.

This is God's desire for you and every believer. He needs your heart postured appropriately and will take care of all the rest. Take the pressure off; you don't need to be great. God is great all by Himself. He wants to use your heart to reflect that greatness. A heart postured from this place will never want to leave. Proper heart posture gives us access to the Kingdom of God. When the Kingdom comes, everything God has is accessible to us! We get the King and access to His Kingdom. When our heart is postured under His authority, we live in an atmosphere of freedom.

RECEIVE THE RAIN

> *"Now the Lord is the Spirit, and where the Spirit of the Lord is, there is freedom."*
> —2 CORINTHIANS 3:17

Have you ever seen rain fall on dry ground so fast that it creates a flood? Our area can be tricky to navigate in times of abundant rain. No one knows how much rain has fallen or how dry the ground was until there's so much water that everything is floating or immersed. When the rain comes to our hearts, it is the same. In comparison, this rain is the imagery of what happens in the Spirit. It is real. You have heard of Him; he is the Holy Spirit. He is the MORE of God that we need. He is God in us.

> *It is important to know that He doesn't just fill you, so you will be satisfied. He fills you to spill you.*

There is never a time that we, as believers, will experience all there is to God. There is always more. He wants us to ask for more.

He is waiting to give us more. He longs for you to have more of Him. The more of the Holy Spirit you have flowing in you, the more things in your life will float and move. Things that used to weigh you down will become light. What seemed impossible to move on your own will be lifted with ease. Shame cannot stick to your heart! The more rain that pours, the more what is in you will come out of you.

We need the rain of the Holy Spirit to fill our lives and overflow. If you are thirsty, He has a limitless supply. Matthew 5:6 says, "Blessed are those who hunger and thirst for righteousness, for they will be filled." If you are thirsty, He will fill you. It is important to know that He doesn't just fill you so you will be satisfied. He fills you to spill you. All you have to do is ask Him for more of His Spirit to flow out of you. If you ask for it and your heart is in the right place, He will open the floodgate of your life, and blessings will flow for His glory.

OPEN THE FLOOD GATE

> *"Freely you have received; freely give."*
> —MATTHEW 10:8

We live near Cherokee Dam. The dam regulates the outflow of water from the Cherokee Lake. That outflow of the dam determines the depth of the lake. When it rains, and the lake fills, what is released is intentional. The water is released as the dam opens, creating power as the flood waters flow appropriately. How amazing is it to think about our hearts in the same way? When the rain of the Holy Spirit has filled our hearts, God can release the overflow to others. When the Holy Spirit flows out of our lives, there is power. Give the controls of your heart gate to the Holy Spirit.

Think of what would happen if there were no outflow. The water would become stagnant and smelly. We would need the rain to stop because the water would not have anywhere to flow, and this would be disastrous for everything attached to the lake. It would spill over negatively. Let the water of the Holy Spirit get what's in you out of you. It's about opening your heart and letting what He has poured in to come out.

Have you ever heard someone tell you a story about someone else's life? I like to listen to people who are gifted storytellers. My dad is one of the best I know. But even the best storyteller on the planet can't share your story in the way that you can. When it's personal, it's authentic. Open the floodgate of your heart and destroy shame. God is glorified, and power is seen through your story. So share it; share it with your words. Share your story through the way you live. Share your story through the relationships you have. Share your story to encourage others and change lives. Open the floodgate and share your story. Allow the power of God through you to change others.

LIVE YOUR PURPOSE

The weight is lifted once shame, fear, doubt, or anything that has held you down has vacated. You will have the freedom to follow the call of God on your life and accomplish His specific purpose for your life.

Let's go back to what we shared at the beginning. What is it about your story that God wants to use? Well, that is simple . . . everything! The longer I journey with Jesus, the more I discover He wants everything. When you are living hidden in Christ, everything is revealed. He wants to use everything! He gets glory for the good and the bad. He wants to use my testimony—the times my faith was tested, and I grew; the times that temptations got the best of me, and I fell. He did not free you to filter you. Shame says it must be polished and pretty before it can be shared. Jesus says, "I paid for your heart with my blood. My mess wins over yours." Nothing that God redeems will ever be wasted. God has proved this to be true over and over again. In His ministry, Jesus changed lives everywhere He went. Changed lives change lives.

> *He did not free you to filter you.*

DRIPPING OIL

My favorite account of when Jesus changed a life was His encounter with Mary Magdalene. There are several Marys mentioned in Scripture, and it sometimes takes work to keep them straight. Mary Magdalene was first mentioned in Luke 8:2, where it says she was delivered from seven demons and healed of diseases. Further study of this scripture reveals that she was from Magdala on the Sea of Galilee. Magdala was a town with great wealth and great evil to go with its wealth. The city was so evil that it was destroyed *because* of its evil. Mary was a prostitute who had great wealth at the time she encountered Jesus. The day she met the healer from Nazareth, her life was changed forever. Once freed, she spent all her wealth on Jesus. She wanted to see others experience the man who changed her past, present, and future.

Mary Magdalene remained a faithful disciple of Jesus throughout His earthly ministry. We see her mentioned as one of the women at the foot of the cross while Jesus was crucified, and she was the first person at the tomb the day He had been resurrected. Jesus commissioned her as the world's first evangelist; she saw and spoke to Him first. He told her to tell the others (John 20:15-18). Mary expressed devotion from a heart completely changed. Here is what makes that scene even more beautiful to me. She was at the tomb to anoint the body of Jesus for burial. So, she went to the tomb with oil.

In Jewish law, oil was mixed with intention. It was also costly and marked moments of real significance. Mary Magdalene brought oils to the tomb. She intended to anoint Jesus. This was an act of gratitude. I can imagine the thoughts that raced through her head. She walked to pay respects to the man who had given her respect the day He met her three years prior. In one last act of service, she walked to anoint Him and say goodbye.

Much to her surprise, she encountered Jesus alive. He told her not to touch Him with the oil; instead, He sent her out to share with others. I have a picture in my mind where Mary is holding the oil out to Jesus, and He turns her hands towards the world. He commissioned her to go and share with others the good news or "drip oil" on the earth. Mary walked, dripping oil of gratitude everywhere as she ran to tell everyone the news. He is not there; the tomb is empty. The One who rescued me—He's alive.

Just as Mary was, we are commissioned to go out with the story of freedom. Go, "drip oil," and change lives with what Jesus has done in you. The oil is your testimony; it is very costly and shows the world what Jesus has done in your life. If He can do it for you, there is hope for them. We cannot be too stingy to share. He has redeemed your heart and set you free from shame. You have a story to tell. You have people to reach; they are waiting on your oil. Show them the price Jesus paid for your freedom, and let oil leave a trail for others to follow—your life's purpose and leading people to freedom. Jesus makes people what they aren't without Him. Your story brings a unique perspective when shared from a heart free from shame.

PRAYER OF COMMITMENT

Thank You, Father, for the freedom I have found because of your Son. I am so thankful that the cross made the way for my freedom. I renounce shame and sin. I declare freedom over my heart. I posture my heart lower, so I can be found in You. I ask You to rain down more of Your Spirit in my life, and open up the floodgates of my life so the world will see You. I want to leave the oil of life change everywhere I go. In Jesus's name, AMEN.

MATTERS OF THE HEART

"In your relationships with one another, have the same mindset as Christ Jesus."
—PHILIPPIANS 2:5

Growing up in a pastor's home meant being socially adaptable. We moved several times, allowing me to grow in my adaptability. The most significant test I faced was attending four different high schools. There is a story behind each move, but that isn't the point. My junior year ended, and my family moved from St. Louis, Missouri, to Akron, Ohio. I was struggling with leaving my entire life behind, and my history teacher could see it. One day before school ended, he asked me to stay after class.

He made a statement to me that has never left me. He said, "You can't see this right now, but this move has a purpose. God wants you there. But if you spend six months leaving where you have been and entering where you are, you could miss it." Life is so much like relationships. Some places we go are seasonal, but there is a purpose. Some seasons will last longer than others, but there is a purpose. Don't get stuck on the season or the timing; stay focused on the purpose. The purpose is about the journey. Open up your heart, embrace the pain, and experience the joy. Then you will know the fullness of the purpose for each place in life."

Such incredible words, and they've stayed with me. It took years to realize the power and strength they spoke into my life. I tried remembering the teacher's name, but couldn't. It didn't matter much, because his purpose in my life was for that one moment—to speak a word that would stick to my heart for the rest of my life. His words about life and relationships are valid.

Some relationships are seasonal. They have different purposes in our lives. Seasonal relationships have various expiration dates and require different levels of accountability and effort. Seasonal people come and go. People who are with you for the long haul are "journey people," and those are the kind of relationships that stay. Journey people are a part of your purpose. The challenge is to decipher whether a person is a journey person or not, all while keeping the ability to be open and appropriately guarded, expect pain, and look for the purpose.

CONSTRUCTING WALLS VS. CREATING SPACE

Relationships are simply about placement. How significant will this person be? How much space will they hold in my heart? What purpose will this person have in my life? How close to my heart should they be? If you are responsible with your heart, you have asked yourself at least one or more of these questions. Evaluation must happen if we are to steward our hearts in our relationships well. An assessment of a relationship at the ground level is needed to determine safety. We must ask: are we creating space or building walls?

The human heart has what we call heart walls. Heart walls are the muscles that contract and relax to create space in the heart chambers. That space is responsible for holding and releasing blood with every heart pump. A certain amount of blood must remain in the chambers to power the pump, and the rest is released to cycle.[41] The danger with the heart wall is that it becomes weak and rigid. It cannot pump like it should, so it keeps too much blood out, and the space in the heart valves decreases. Then, it doesn't pump strongly enough, so the blood flow in and out is significantly limited.

How's that for powerful imagery of a relationship?!?! We are using the wisdom of boundaries to build appropriate walls. These walls intentionally create space. The walls divide your heart into sections. Some relationships stay on the outside of the heart, and some are needed to power the innermost parts of your heart. The walls instinctively know when relationships need to move or change. So, the walls release some and then pull in others. Their muscle strength has created space for what is needed and knows what is not. That is the power of wisdom at work in our lives. Damaged walls can be dangerous because they can become defensive and closed. When we have been "hurt," we try to use those walls to keep people out and won't let anyone else in. It becomes detrimental to our survival. We need people in our lives. The relationship walls in our hearts are to make space for others with good boundaries. Walls built on damage keep people out, and that kind of damage will kill us. Refrain from constructing walls in defense. Create space with boundaries.

BOUNDARIES WITHIN THE HEART

Relational hurt is a challenging topic to discuss sometimes. Jesus blew up any chance of us not allowing people into our lives when He told us that first, we are to love Him, and second, we are to love our neighbor as ourselves. People are the most important thing to Jesus, so people need to be the most important thing to

---
[41] "Heart," *Cleveland Clinic*, accessed June 26, 2024, https://my.clevelandclinic.org/health/body/21704-heart.

us. Christ commissions us to love all people. We are to reach all people. The extroverts are cheering now, and the introverts might be running for cover.

All sounds like a lot, Melissa; yes, I know. But all means all. I am naturally an extrovert, so I love being with people and watching them interact with others. I pay attention to this because people are important to me. We should be intentional about seeing people. I want to make sure no one feels unimportant. Their value is unmatched, not just to me, but to their Creator.

Have you ever known a person who has never met a stranger? They carry on conversations with anybody-anywhere, and it's enjoyable. I have several people like that, but Amy is one of my favorites to watch in action. She and her husband, Brandon, moved to Tennessee in 2016. Brandon has been our friend since college, and we got to know his wife, Amy, after we hired Brandon as our worship pastor.

To know Amy is to know laughter. She is the person I am not allowed to sit next to in a quiet setting because we have too much fun. She is witty and never misses an opportunity to make off-the-cuff statements. I get uncomfortable when moments are too intense. (Yes, laughter is a defense mechanism to keep me from feelings that are too vulnerable and raw.)

Amy has a genuine love for people. One day, she shared what she felt called to do, and her words stuck with me. I will paraphrase it: she asked God what He wanted her to do. She has so many talents, but she felt at that time like none were for her to use. She said it dawned on her that she could focus all her efforts on loving people. We are about six years from when I heard her say that, and she is excelling. She loves people, and people love her. Amy recognizes when people are hurting and notices when they are happy. She observes their behaviors, mannerisms, and conversations. She will help them carry burdens, give them a place to belong, and call them out when they need loving accountability.

The reward of love is not always to receive love in return but an act of obedience to God.

Now that you know a little bit about Amy, I know it won't surprise you that she is in charge of creating a place for people to belong. She is our life group director and excels at doing life with people. She does that while raising three awesome kids! I know she would tell you that people have hurt her, disappointed her, and sometimes walked away. I have seen it happen. But there is one thing I have never seen her do. She has never built walls to keep people out of her heart. Instead, I have seen her create boundaries to protect herself and others.

Following Amy's example, I suggest loving people and making people feel seen and valued. The reward of love is not always to receive love in return but an act of obedience to God. Obedience doesn't always guarantee our desired outcome; sometimes, its purpose is to teach us faithfulness to God and not to our desires. The key to relationships and loving all people is to create healthy and appropriate boundaries to protect our hearts and theirs.

Creating healthy and appropriate boundaries is a challenge, even when you have seen good boundaries enforced throughout life. But it can be incredibly challenging if you didn't grow up seeing healthy relationships and boundaries. No matter which category you find yourself in, you can do this. You must do this to have a healthy heart. Relational heart health is vital. We were created to need one another. Healthy relationships provide a safe place for our hearts to rest. Learn how to guard your heart best and make an appropriate space for people.

heart space
THESE SPACES DEFINED

ACQUAINTANCES
LARGE GROUPS OF PEOPLE WHO HAVE LIMITED INTERACTIONS WITH. PEOPLE YOU KNOW OF OR KNOW YOU.

FRIENDS + FAMILY
FRIENDS/FAMILY YOU HAVE INTERACTION WITH FOR SPECIFIED PURPOSE. YOU KNOW THEM AND THEY KNOW YOU BECAUSE OF COMMON INVOLVEMENT OR INTEREST.

CLOSEST FRIENDS + FAMILY
CONSISTENT INTERACTIONS. CLOSE IN RELATIONSHIP. HAVE A KNOWLEDGE OF YOU AND YOU OF THEM ON A DEEPER LEVEL. THEIR LIVES, WORDS AND ACTIONS HOLD SIGNIFICANT WEIGHT IN YOUR LIFE.

CLOSEST RELATIONSHIPS
DAILY INTERACTIONS. THEY SHAPE YOUR LIFE AND INVITE YOU TO SHAPE THEIRS. THIS DEPTH COMES WITH THE HIGHEST TRUST OF YOUR MOST INTIMATE THOUGHTS, FEELINGS AND EMOTIONS. EVERY PART OF LIFE IS SHARED.

TRADING SPACES

In college, there was a popular home renovation show called *Trading Spaces*. In the show, two families who needed a remodel would switch homes and work with an interior designer for the other family's remodel. They had to give complete trust and open their lives to perfect strangers. In doing this, the strangers moved into the most personal space in their lives: their home. If agreed upon, they would trade spaces and assume the project for the other family.[42] I loved watching it. They always came up with creative and beautiful designs. For the most part, the families were happy they participated.

I get entirely nauseous when I think of someone I don't know being in my space. My home is my happy place. The outside world is our place of service to others. My home is a place of service to my family

---
42 *Trading Spaces,* October 13, 2000; TLC and Discovery Channel), television.

and the close friends and family I invite in. It is healthy for your home to be your safe space, especially when you live your life under public scrutiny. The visual of heart spaces may seem elementary to you. It may have blown your mind to think about the space the people in your life occupy. You may have never thought about boundaries or seen them defined. Whatever the case, we should take time and evaluate. You can ask yourself these questions to determine who is filling your heart space:

- Where should this person's space be?
- How do I create boundaries in each space?
- Which space should I invest in the most?
- How much weight and importance does each person carry?

If you are serious about guarding your heart, you have to take inventory of who is taking up space there. Let's define each of those spaces and the rules that keep a person within them. This will help answer most of the questions above. Here are the four layers and how I define them, listed from the outside in.

ACQUAINTANCES

You're walking through the grocery store and the lady in the aisle who just passed you and waved looks familiar. You turn around and quickly access the invisible contact list in your mind, and realize she is the mother of one of the kids your son used to play ball with. Now what? Your following response will depend on your personality. Most extroverts will find the person, say "Hi," explain that it took them a moment to recognize who they were, talk for a few minutes, and leave. The introverts would stop with a smile and a wave, giving themselves bonus points if they also said, "Hi."

Either of those responses is appropriate. Acquaintances are stacked in large quantities for some of us. There are no bad feelings; they aren't a part of your everyday life. Acquaintances can be people you know because of a connection to other people. Possibly, you know them from social media, and that is it. This category is as ambiguous and broad as it is in number. I am acquainted with some incredible people, but that is the depth of our relationship: recognition only.

Healthy boundaries and mindsets are essential for acquaintances because these relationships are outside the heart. Boundaries should be clearest at this level than at any other. You wouldn't run up to this lady at the grocery store and share family information. An acquaintance isn't someone with whom you have any authentic trust; therefore, there should be no weight to their words or statements in our lives. Taking heed of this would save people a lot of stress in their online interactions and battles.

FRIENDS AND FAMILY

Person A: Our neighborhood has regular gatherings four times a year. I enjoy talking to a neighbor who lives near me at those gatherings. If there are ever any issues in the neighborhood, we talk. When we see one another out walking, we stop for small talk, but that is the extent of our friendship.

Person B: Great Aunt Sally sees me every two years at the family reunion. She is always kind, and I love to hear her stories about her life growing up. I look forward to seeing her, but we don't speak in between. Still, I am proud to have her as my family.

Person C: You serve with Joe on a church volunteer team. You see and interact with him weekly, but there is no outside interaction if it doesn't involve church (your common interest).

All parties above are considered friends and family because we have spent time together. We know things about each other that connect us as more than acquaintances. People, experiences, and memories connect us. It would be right to call that person a friend. However, there are still boundaries at the level of distinctly distant relationships.

We know enough about each other to discover similar interests, learn about each other's families, or discover some surface-level information. Relationships in this space have a minimum level of trust. These friends' words and actions hold a little weight.

CLOSE FRIENDS AND FAMILY

These are the people with whom we have consistent interactions. You will call these friends to go to lunch when you need to talk. The family that isn't in the center circle of your heart still dramatically influences your life. Close people know you on a deeper level than just the surface, and you know them. They are in your circle of trust. You value their opinions and actions. If a person in this space needs help, you will do everything you can to make sure and lend them a hand. They are regular texters. You know their story, and they know yours. You have chosen to invest in them, and they make equal investments in you. These are journey people in your life; they pray for and encourage you. They care when there are times to celebrate, and they will cry with you when you are grieving. Your heart is at home with these people; you can be yourself. There is an excellent level of trust in this group. This group of people holds a significant amount of weight in your life.

CLOSEST RELATIONSHIPS

The most important people in my life. They occupy the closest space in my heart. These are people whom I guard, and they guard me. This level is the space with the deepest level of trust. They know you intimately; their hearts house your most profound emotions of joy, sadness, pain, and triumph. They are the first people you call with great news. These relationships are the shoulders you weep on in times of heartbreak. These are the ones mandated by God to sharpen you and them. Everything in your life is open to these relationships and perspectives. These are distance journey people. They know where you have been, where you are, and where you dream of going. Their hearts are intertwined with yours. If you are blessed to have these relationships, you want to guard them because they will profoundly impact the core of your heart.

Now that we have established these four spaces of relationship in our lives, I want to address the two spaces that are the closest to our hearts—who they are, why God has entrusted them to our lives, and why we have been deposited into theirs. So, before we jump in, I need you to understand this truth before anything else: who you are connected to matters! The people in the most interior spaces of your heart will profoundly impact your life.

GUARDING THE HEART OF MARRIAGE

Who you marry matters. It is the second most important decision you will make in your entire life. (The most critical decision is to put your faith in Christ.) Ephesians 5:25-33 compares the heart of Christ towards the church to a husband-and-wife relationship. No other relationship is described as *holy*, save a marriage between man and woman. So, if this relationship is holy, our hearts should seek particular character. Christ affirmed the importance of this relationship, and its importance cannot be overstated. What should you find in the heart of the person you marry?

If they don't share your love for God, they cannot share you with Him.

A HEART FOR GOD

This is a nonnegotiable to having a covenant that is God-honoring. How can you unite as one with a person who doesn't understand your allegiance to God the Father?

If they don't share your love for God, they cannot share you with Him. If a potential spouse does not understand your need, love, and longing for a relationship with Christ, then there can be no oneness with you. What's more of a deal breaker than being unequally yoked? Nothing. Second Corinthians 6:14 asks the best question: "For what do righteousness and wickedness have in common? Or what fellowship can light have with darkness?" God desires to bless the couple who share in oneness and the world around them. When there is no agreement in Christ, all will be lacking.

In the last twenty years, we have met with dozens of couples. They sit in tears before us as they share the betrayal and unfaithfulness that has intruded on the heart of the marriage. In 100 percent of the cases, love and obedience to God were missing in the partner who caused the indiscretion. We have seen God do miracles and turn the hearts of the husbands and wives back to one another and back to Him. We have seen beautiful redemption stories when this has happened, but it sometimes goes differently. Just as often, one or both spouses are missing the one vital ingredient for healing and restoration: forgiveness. How could you forgive yourself or one another properly if you do not know the life-changing forgiveness of Christ?

Love for Christ is a nonnegotiable. You need to see this fruit alive in the person's life before you marry them. And if you are reading this and are already married before you had this knowledge, there is hope. Pray, fast, and ask God to pursue your spouse's heart. Ask Him to use your love to show Christ's love to your spouse. Doing your part to ensure the person you marry loves God more than they love you solves many potential marriage problems. When my spouse falls short of my expectations of him, his love for the Lord keeps me without fear. When I fall short of my spouse's expectations, he can trust my love for the Lord and live in peace. When the most vital thing between you is your love and commitment to Jesus, you have a solid foundation. This way, your oneness will be rooted in Christ and not one another.

Remember, you will raise children with this person. If faith and love for Christ aren't first, this will be extremely difficult to cultivate in your children's lives. It's not impossible, just challenging. I have witnessed so many men and women who get engaged and think they can change their chosen person—I assure you; it doesn't happen. Choose the heart with which you connect in marriage wisely. That person will occupy a space that no one else should and their heart will become one with yours.

> *I guard what I treasure — we don't treasure what we don't guard!*

....

YOUR HEART ABOVE MY OWN

Justin and I have been married for twenty-one years. (I am still determining how that happened; we have yet to age one bit!) I can tell you, hands down, they have been twenty-one beautiful years. We have gone through many difficult seasons. Seasons when the road seemed long, dark, and winding, but we made it through. We have gone through many beautiful seasons. Seasons of joy, laughter, and strength; we enjoyed every moment.

We have learned many things in the twenty-three years we have been together, and one of the most important is that when we fight hell for each other, we fight less with each other. I will protect my spouse's heart and, in doing so, protect the call of God on his life. I guard what I treasure—we don't treasure what we don't guard! It is my calling to stand over his heart and take out the enemy before they even reach the gate. He is my best friend; he is my partner. First Corinthians 13 is the "Love chapter" and says that love always protects and trusts.

Ministry and marriage can be an adventure. You always encounter people who are hurting and have no boundaries, and then some are just plain demonic. I don't have a jealous bone in my body, but I am protective of the people I love. In our first year of pastoring, while trying to love the community and grow the church, we stayed busy. We were raising two kids who were still adjusting to the move to Tennessee. We both worked outside the church, organizing and training people in our free time. One lady started coming to the church and was coming around a lot. We were getting to know her, and as far as we could tell, she was a good person.

Then, one night, Justin's phone went off. He picked it up and said, "Ugh, here you go. I think she sent this to me by mistake." After handing me the phone, I realized the woman in our church had sent him a video, through social media, of herself talking to him while lying in bed, inappropriately dressed, and telling him he was a wonderful pastor (gross)! We understood what was happening then, and I entered full heart protection mode (not today, devil)! I immediately sent her a message and invited her to lunch the following day. She fumbled around the answer but finally agreed.

I am sure she didn't know what to expect when I arrived calm and collected. I explained to her that Justin handed his phone to me as soon as he saw a video and that I was the one who watched it, not him. We keep no secrets, and she found that out fast. I told her she was not welcome to make advances towards him ever again. I welcomed her back to church, and she continued to call me for prayer and pastoral assistance. Lunch was short. She stuck it out with us for about another six months, and then we never saw her again. Although the attacks come from all sides and look different, we are eleven years past that moment, still guarding one another's hearts above our own. I will protect him at all costs. I will not allow the enemy to weaken the gate of his heart. Not on my watch.

GUARDING THE HEARTS OF OUR CHILDREN

I see things differently now after having spent nine years in youth ministry and raising teenagers. I have witnessed parents go before me and model what incredible parenting looks like, and I have seen just as many fall asleep at the wheel of parenting and end up in a ditch of destruction. So, what is the catch? How do we raise great kids who are well-rounded, love God, and are ready for life? The home you raise your children in matters. It matters how they see you live. For example, you model marriage by the way you treat your spouse. While we cannot always control their choices, we can control their environment. If you are a single parent or divorced and looking to remarry, it matters who you choose to bring into the lives of your children.

The Word of God is our measuring stick for parenting, not the world. This means we make calls regarding the safety of our children's minds, bodies, and souls based on God's standards. We are their gatekeepers. When the rest of the world gave phones and social media to eight and nine-year-olds, we chose to wait. Our kids got a cell phone when they entered high school, and our daughter just got social media as a senior in high school. I could write a book on the safeguards we put up out of love.

Before you think we are "sheltering" them, let me confirm that we do—in all the ways that matter. We have chosen to shelter them from the enemy who prowls and waits to devour their souls. We protect them from the evil that lurks behind the seemingly innocent things that "everyone is doing." We work hard to ensure they focus on what they are given instead of what they aren't permitted to do. We explain to them why we draw boundaries and make certain decisions.

We are involved with our children. We talk to them and make sure they know that our door is always open to them. There is no question that we won't answer or conversation we shy away from. We are committed to guarding the hearts of our children. One day, we will stand before our Creator and be held accountable. On that day, we will answer for what we taught them by what we allowed and didn't allow. God will hold us responsible for disciplining and pulling out sin and rebellion from our homes rather than pointing out the sin and allowing it to continue. As parents, we hold the most significant place in our children's lives—the opportunity to steward their souls. We can set them up for success in life.

As I wrapped up the parenting section, I asked my daughter to write how it felt growing up with parents who guarded her heart. She just turned eighteen, and she is great with words and honest with her feelings. This was her response:

"You're just a teenager, you wouldn't understand."
"You're just a kid; you will grow out of it."
"What can you do about it? You're too young."

These are the words adults tell many teenagers today. I have watched these seemingly harmless words destroy many of my peers. It has broken my heart to see many of my friends fall into the pit of their problems, feeling as if no one cared about what they were going through. I watched as many of my friends turned to things other than God for a false sense of joy that would only last ten seconds. All of this is because they lacked godly involvement and influence from the adults in their lives.

However, I got lucky. I was blessed with a mom and dad who didn't brush off my problems, partly because they are also my pastors. I had a fantastic mom who quickly became my free-of-charge therapist when life became rocky in my middle school years. She was my life vest in the raging waters of anxiety. But most importantly, she taught me how to trust God to carry me throughout my life. She taught me how important it is to follow the voice of God no matter what the world might tell me. She is my rock, a person of strength for me and everyone around her.

I was also blessed with my dad. He is my mentor, my biggest fan, and the comedic relief in my life. He taught me how to live my life with integrity because it honors God and the calling God has for me. He has cheered me on and believed in me when it was hard to believe in myself. He has brought me joy by making me laugh so hard my ribs physically hurt!

So why am I bragging about my parents this much? Simple. To bring it back to what I started with: I don't know where I would be today if I didn't have their influence in my life. They guarded me. Looking back on my high school, middle school, and elementary school years, I realize that my parents' goal was never for me to make it through life with no problems. They didn't "shelter" me, in the way some people would say. They didn't hide me from all the bad things in life. They did something even better. They showed me how to take what life throws at me and walk straight through it. Want some examples?

I previously mentioned that throughout middle school, I dealt with a lot of anxiety. That was the biggest battle I have ever had to overcome. I would sometimes stay up all night worrying myself to death with things that didn't even matter in the long run. I remember that my mom intentionally poured into me during all of this. She would come into my room with the tissues for my tears and sit until I felt better. But she didn't allow me to stay in that place. I remember one night, I was at it again. My anxiety was through the roof, and into my room came my mother with her phone. She sat down just like the other times, but a song began to play through her speaker this time. I remember sitting there listening to this worship song and feeling a peace I can't explain. Later in life, I realized what she had done. She showed me the best weapon against any attack from the enemy was worship. My mother was guarding my heart for me until I could learn to guard it on my own, but she realized that she would have to teach me how to do that.

I tell you that story to urge you to show the next generation how to guard their hearts starting at a young age to become everything God has called them to be. It is time to intentionally raise them in the ways God has laid out for us. They need you. They need you to put up guardrails that they cannot put up for themselves. They need you to operate the lock and key. I see it now; my parents were guarding what got in because they cared about the outcome.

I am eighteen. I am going off to college. I am going to start a life of my own. I know what it was like to feel inadequate because of my age. The enemy is attacking the minds of young people now more than ever before because he knows what we are capable of. I remember feeling as if I weren't brave enough to face God's call on my life. However, my parents and mentors intentionally poured into me and trained me to fulfill God's plan for my life. And I am grateful for that. I am thankful for a family who raised me to be a woman of God, full of wisdom and confidence.

It is time for the family to get in their gates. Raising the next generation is hard (believe me, I know I was not always easy to parent), but that is the point. We are young. We are malleable. We are learning. Therefore, godly adults need to pour their love into us wholeheartedly. Just because we are young does not mean we are inadequate. First Timothy puts it wonderfully, "Let no one despise you for your youth, but set the believers an example in speech, in conduct, in love, in faith, in purity" (1 Timothy 4:12, ESV). When you look down and ignore the potential of the next generation, it makes it hard for them to learn how to use the gifts God gave them.

Every teenager is looking for something. They know that there is immeasurably more waiting for them in life, but when trusted adults overlook their struggles, they can't find where they are meant to be. In most of my struggles, I never reached out and asked my mom and dad for help. Somehow, they just knew. They were watching my heart. My mom and dad instinctively saw what even I could not. On more than one occasion, they've told me, "We are going to be accountable to God for how we guard your heart." I am grateful they took their job seriously.

I have watched as my friends turn to things that could eventually kill them all because they lack guidance in their lives. I have watched them fall entirely away from the faith because they felt they didn't measure up or no one seemed to care enough to stop them. I have watched younger *people that I know overdose on vapes and turn to sexual sins because they want someone or something to fill the void in their hearts that only Jesus can fill. I have watched adults overlook what should be their biggest priority—their family. I have seen teen after teen lose sight of God because their heart was compromised. I see it now: they needed a "guardian." Every child and teenager needs one. I will always be grateful I had two of them.*

GUARDING THE HEARTS OF A COVENANT FRIENDSHIP

The greatest gift a person can give another is the gift of friendship. The type of friendship that touches the core of your heart is beautiful. Proverbs 27:17 tells us that friendship is like iron sharpening iron, and I can attest that true friends make life so enjoyable. Throughout this book, I have written about a lot of my friends. Allow me to share the two types of friends you want to have in your life.

LIFETIME FRIENDS

I am aware that these types of friends are few and very rare. When you find them, you should value them. A lifetime friend has seen you through every season of life—the good, the bad, and the ugly. They never walk away. Proverbs 17:17 says: "A friend loves at all times, and a brother is born for a time of adversity." This scripture tells us love is always present in this friendship. This friend rises to another level when you face the toughest struggles and overcome them together. A lifetime friend can see you at your worst and believe in the best. They can look past your moments of craziness; they see your flaws, but they know your heart. These types of friends are rare. So, if you have one, be grateful. I know I sure am.

I am blessed to have such a friend who has been with me all my life. She came into the world seventeen months before me, in the same house. She is my only sibling, my sister, Kimberly. Growing up, we were close. During our teenage years, we took a break so we wouldn't choke each other. But once she left for college, we were closer than before, and continue to be. Together, we have been through heartbreak, pain, accomplishments, and joy, and we have seen each other through to the other side. From raising kids to leading churches, we have many things in common. I am thankful for the gift she is to me. While we haven't always agreed or seen eye-to-eye on things, we have always stayed close. She is beautiful, intelligent, and has more style than a New York runway model. But the most significant part about her is her love for God. She has made me a better person all my life just by being in my life. My favorite thing is the consistent laughter that we share! Anytime we talk or are together, laughter is always present. Kim and I hold space in each other's history, and we believe in one another's destiny. She lives in Ohio, and I am in Tennessee, but we still walk through life together.

Lifetime friends don't have to talk daily (but it's fun when we get to); we are joined at the heart. Our lives intertwined throughout a lifetime of memories. Because of the place she holds, we can say things to each other that we wouldn't allow anyone else to say. We aren't going anywhere; we are here for life. I will be her loudest cheerleader, die-hard fan, and prayer covering. She holds space in my heart that no one else can. God blessed us to be sisters, but we choose to be friends. And that is a relationship that no one can come between.

JOURNEY PARTNERS

The difference between lifetime friends and journey partners is that journey partners have joined you at a pivotal point. I call them seasons of increase. You didn't see these friendships coming, but now that they are here, you can't imagine life without them. The other day, while listening to *The Bible Recap*, the host, Tara Leigh Cobble, read Proverbs 27:6: "Wounds from a friend can be trusted, but an enemy multiplies kisses." She then asked, "Who have you invited to righteously wound you?" And I thought of my journey partners. Because of the level of trust and respect, they are invited to speak into my life differently. I have allowed them into a space that few people are, into my weakness and vulnerability. They are unique and God-sent. These relationships cannot be forced; they are only forged.

Trusting you in this space allows you to see my weakness, call it out, and challenge me. That's concrete, and I need that! Vulnerability puts me on edge. If I am being transparent, vulnerability isn't a place I like to be. It's uncomfortable, feels a bit intrusive, draws too much attention to me, and requires too much emotion. (It is interesting since I have a counseling degree and know how to pull it out of others, but I struggle expressing it myself.) Because you are reading this book, you will now know more than 80 percent of the people in my life know about me. Welcome to my living room! It's easy to share my heart with you because I don't get a response to what I write. We can skip the awkward moments of not knowing what to say or the forced questions.

I welcome everyone else's vulnerability; I would love to hear your story. Until the season I went through after COVID-19, I barely could even cry. (The one emotion you will know I feel is joy.) I am not heartless, just not an extremely emotional woman. I was locked up tight, protecting my heart from being known, out of habit. I spend my life listening to others and am okay with not being heard. I have a prayer life and a fantastic husband. What more could I need? (Or so I thought) I remember the day that everything changed.

One night, going through the valley of anxiety, I felt the Lord ask me, *Who knows you?* He then challenged me to invite some prayer warriors into my life and allow them to get to know me. One by one, the Holy Spirit showed me who to ask. Before I knew it, I had four of the fiercest women on Earth fighting for me. They were there to pray with me through the darkest moments and are still beside me today. They've got my back, and I have theirs. It is not one-sided. We are a team. I know them and lift up their families and needs. They pray over me before I preach at The Avenue or elsewhere. When they are able, they travel with me to speaking engagements. They are my journey people and the devil's worst nightmare. Ecclesiastes 4:12 says, "Though one may be overpowered, two can defend themselves. A cord of three strands is not quickly broken." I trust these ladies. What I share with them is never talked about; it's prayed about. They have brought so much to my life.

You cannot and should not do life alone. No matter who you are or how strong and independent you are, we all need journey people. Last year, we hosted our first Guarded Women's Conference and introduced the Journey Partner Program for any lady who needs someone to journey with them through a growing season. We have a long list of partners that we paired with people in need. We will continue to believe that we are stronger together. God has and continues to use journey partners to change people's lives. Real-life change happens in the context of relationships. This is a friend who really knows you where you are and believes for where you are headed.

HEART CONNECTIONS

God has given us different relationships for different spaces in our hearts. We have to determine the people and their placements. Be efficient in taking inventory of the people with whom you are connected. Ensure they are connections that God wants for you to continue. Evaluate their space in your heart and adjust what you feel prompted to adjust.

> *Don't build walls to keep people out; build them to give people space, value, and capacity.*

Our responsibility is to provide stewardship over the hearts of those who are the most deeply connected to our hearts. We are responsible for creating the most space for our marriages, children, and/or closest friends. Don't build walls to keep people out; build them to give people space, value, and capacity. The relationships in your life will have a profound impact on your heart because all relationships are *Matters of the Heart,* and it is your heart that matters in relationships. Guard your heart. Guard the spaces of your heart. Guard the boundaries of your heart. Guard the people in your heart.

PRAYER OF COMMITMENT

Father, take the wrong people out of my life and bring the right people into it—people that are going to push me closer to You. I surrender all my walls and relationships to You. Have Your way in me, in Jesus's name, AMEN.

LEADERS WHO FALL

"Not so with you. Instead, whoever wants to become great among you must be your servant."
—MARK 10:43

Once our hearts are stewarded well, we can lead others well. A heart that leads from any other place leaves the leader, followers, and entire organization susceptible to downfall and defeat. I'm sure this is the last thing anyone wants. I have been a long-time student of Dr. John Maxwell; he is known for his statement, "Leadership is influence, nothing more, nothing less."[43] Influence is the bedrock of leadership. I have often seen it: influential people become the pack's leader. The question we must answer then becomes, "From where does their influence derive?" I bet you know now, and you've already said it—THE HEART. Influence comes from the overflow of a leader's heart.

---

43 John C. Maxwell, *The 21 Irrefutable Laws of Leadership: Follow Them and People Will Follow You* (Nashville, TN: HarperCollins Leadership, 2007).

WE ARE ALL LEADERS

"All are leaders" is not a statement to give everyone a pat on the back. I am not dubbing you "leader of the year," nor am I assuming that I know your life. We all have areas of life that depend on our influence. No matter how great or small, people depend on the leadership flowing from the heart. You don't have to have a title, be high profile, or bring in a big paycheck to be a leader. (If you have those things, that is great.) You may see your role as a leader as insignificant or "not a big deal." I encourage you to open your heart to a more profound truth.

Let's look at influence and where it flows from. Influence is "the effect somebody/something has on the way a person thinks or behaves or on the way something works or develops."[44] Based on this definition, that means anyone who interacts with people. You might not see your effect on others, but you have an impact. Whether or not that effect is positive or negative depends on your heart. We are leading the people we are responsible for somewhere with the life that flows from our hearts. Real always shows; it is only a matter of time before people see a person's true heart. Leaders' influence and ability will only be as strong as their source: the heart—their source of life and their fountain for leadership.

INCONVENIENCE VS. INCARCERATION

Love it or hate it, we will never be able to produce long-term, outstanding leadership from a blemished or compromised heart. An unhealthy heart can cause more damage than can even be calculated. Leadership influence is like dropping a rock in the water and trying to decipher the place where the water stops moving. I can tell you it's not possible. Even if you cannot see the ripple moving from

---

[44] *Oxford Advanced Learner's Dictionary*, s.v. "influence," accessed June 27, 2024, https://www.oxfordlearnersdictionaries.com/us/definition/english/influence_1.

the point of impact, the movement of the water has already affected the water on the shore. Leadership causes movement, be it good or bad. The size of the rock will determine the splash and the length of the waves, but the water is still disturbed.

From something as small as leading the snack schedule for the little league baseball team to leading a Fortune 500 company, your influence impacts others. The only difference between the two roles is the detriment of what that impact causes. Suppose you are the snack leader of the little league baseball team, responsible for assigning someone to bring drinks, but you forget. The effect is an *inconvenience*. You or someone else will have to get drinks, or the kids will be thirsty. If you are leading a Fortune 500 company and forget to assign someone to pay the taxes to the IRS, the impact is *incarceration* or jail time. See the difference? Both consequences are felt, but their impact will vary significantly. That brings a new insight: "The bigger they are, the harder they fall."

> *Fall on your face before Jesus before you fall on your face in failure.*

No matter the level you lead, your influence will be felt. Your responsibility will be to guard and grow your hearts to the level needed. You can only hide your heart and fake the front for so long before the contents of your heart (or the lack thereof) spill out. So, my best advice to every leader at every level is to fall on your face before Jesus before you fall on your face in failure.

FALL ON YOUR FACE

When you live your life leading people, there will be times you wish you could go back and undo. Like in the movie *Back to the Future*,[45] you want your future self to warn your past self of unforeseen dangers. Even though I have learned far more from my failures and falls than I have ever learned from my successes, failure isn't pleasant. But it is a great teacher.

Each year in November, we host our annual Thanksgiving meal giveaway at The Avenue. It's a big deal. We invite hundreds of families in need to come and get a turkey and all the ingredients they need to cook a meal for their family on Thanksgiving. In November 2017, the giveaway arrived, and the church auditorium was jam-packed with people. I was on the worship team that day, and our stage had limited space. My husband loves to use illustrations when he preaches, which is a great touch, but adding that to the stage made movement nearly impossible. (This was in our second stage of facility growth, so the space was about one-third the size we are today—that stage was a far cry from our current stage.)

Worship ended, and the lights came down to begin the announcement video. The stage was solid black, and the room was in blackout mode. It was a recipe for a disaster. The light from the video illuminated the stage enough for us to see the side stairs. Loading all the musicians and vocalists off the stage had to happen quickly so the team could set the props before the lights came up. Where I stood on the stage meant everyone needed to go before me before I could put the mic down and get off. It took longer than usual, so the props team moved them on while the team was exiting to ensure they were

---
[45] Robert Zemeckis, *Back to the Future* (July 3, 1985; Universal City, CA: Universal Pictures).

placed in time. With props in the way, I couldn't get to the side with the handrail, so I had to go down the front steps.

I was thirty-five then, so these were still the days of wearing fabulous shoes, even when they felt like torture devices. Beauty is pain! I had high-heeled boots on, and as I headed down the stairs, the heel of my left foot got caught on the top step. Because there was no railing to grab onto, I tried to correct myself by using the heel to grab onto the step, but I failed. The moment I turned, I felt a snap in my knee, followed by five seconds of intense pain. The pain was right up there with active labor; it took my breath away. Focused on the pain, I knew I was falling and had to think fast. I was going down five stairs onto a concrete floor. I had to decide what would do the least amount of damage to my already injured self. In a split-second decision, I decided to fall on the knee that was already wounded, so that is precisely what I did. No one saw me to catch me because the lights were out, and everything happened so fast. Even my husband, sitting on the first row, was surprised when I landed full force. My daughter, who was ten and highly emotional at the time, threw her body over mine and just started wailing big crocodile tears. Face down on the floor, I got a few people's attention, and they carried me out. But not before the video ended. When the lights came up, I was in full view of 320 onlookers, all as shocked as I was about what had happened.

Embarrassing, right?! Embarrassment was the last thing on my mind due to all the pain I was in and all the people that I had distracted from service. After tests and scans, it was confirmed that the pain I felt first was my ACL snapping in two, followed by another injury—a torn MCL and meniscus that had lodged in my joint, preventing me from bending it—when I hit the floor. All injuries would require surgery and months of healing to function like usual again. It's a crazy story, but it happened. It was painful and costly, and it interrupted my life and that of others. That day, a lot of things changed. I haven't worn high-heeled shoes since that moment. Our stage is different. The room is different, and even how we enter and exit the stage is different.

> *He watches as we choose to scar our hearts and the hearts of others by forsaking that freedom.*

I learned so much through that journey. The memories of the pain I experienced and the inconvenience I caused others are still fresh in my mind. My knee is doing fantastic now. I haven't had a moment of trouble since I was 100 percent healed. However, falling changed me. I think about my feet when I walk. I am careful every time I am on a stage. I have moments where I remember the pain I endured and thank God that it came to an end. But my daily reminders are the scars I have as evidence of the fall.

The experience of falling off a stage is strangely similar to when leaders fall from positions of significant influence and power. From the marketplace and courthouse to the church house, the fall of a leader is painful. I will speak to ministry because that is the world I live in. News outlets are regularly reporting other ministry scandals—another man or woman who has fallen detrimentally. Another pastor or leader who has abused power and fallen. The rug is finally too bumpy to keep sins hidden. By the time the fallen leader hits the concrete, onlookers are in shock and disbelief. A fall of this nature destroys the hearts of those connected to the leader in any way. The ripples extend far beyond those directly impacted. No one can anticipate their reach. No one saw it coming! But is that really true? I know One who did. His name is Jesus. The One who bears the scars for our freedom. He watches as we choose to scar our hearts and the hearts of others by forsaking that freedom.

James 1:14-15 says, "But each person is tempted when they are dragged away by their own evil desire and enticed. Then, after desire has conceived, it gives birth to sin; and sin, when it is full-grown, gives birth to death." Christ just told us in the book of James how and why leaders fall. The enemy throws temptation out until he knows what turns your head. He only knows what entices you because he watched what you had an appetite for the time before. And once he finds what gets you, he will use it repeatedly until you have a full-blown case of habitual sin. Remember, the root of habitual sin is pride, and pride comes before a fall. In 100 percent of the cases of hidden and habitual sin in any leader, this is the problem. But for every situation, there is an answer: 1 Corinthians 10: 11-13. Let me explain. The Word says everyone will face temptation. We must be careful so we do not fall. Then He said He would provide your way of escape. What is that escape? Fall at His feet before you fall to sin.

Fall on your face before Him daily, so you don't fail those who follow you.

As a leader, you have to follow the same plan. Lay down your pride, selfish desires, and the sin that gets you all tangled up. Fall on your face at His feet and surrender your heart to Him. Move your heart to a lower level; hidden in Christ, so you can escape any temptation. Fall on your face in prayer before the Creator of your heart. He is the source of power and all that your heart needs. Fall on your face in humility. Ask Him to search your heart and forgive you of all your selfishness. Allow Him to pull out of you anything that could cause you to fall. Fall on your face before Him daily, so you don't fail those who follow you. Falling on your face ensures that your eyes are on what matters: Him. If our eyes are on Him, our hearts and leadership will look like His. We will realize that anything good in us is Him. Our heart beats as one with Him when we stay on our faces before Jesus. If I step out of rhythm, He will correct me so I don't fall before man.

We have to consider the following areas to determine if our hearts are postured to lead like Jesus:

SERVANTHOOD

Humility was the hallmark of Jesus's ministry on Earth (Mark 10:45). He lived it with every exchange, every message, every healing, and every criticism. Humility flowed from Jesus's heart. He was never prideful, arrogant, or a know-it-all. Jesus knew He came to do the will of His Father in heaven, and His heart was postured to serve. His heart of compassion for people was evident; He even cared enough to teach His disciples to do the same. He led by example, so He created servant-minded disciples. Jesus knew this very pivotal truth: you will never create around you the type of leaders you want; you will only develop around you the kind of leaders you are.

You reproduce who you are. If your heart as a leader isn't postured to serve, then those who serve with you won't prioritize it. We lead a church with thousands of people, and you will still find us occasionally cleaning a bathroom and taking out trash. We have to sneak it now or fight our staff team, but we must do it because it's healthy for our hearts. It is a reminder of the heart of the One we serve. I've heard it said before, "If you are too important to serve, you are too important to lead." One of the tests of authentic leadership in a person's heart is this: will you do the job that no one else wants to do? And can you do it with such an incredible heart that others want to do it with you? If so, God can use you. Skills can be taught; I would take a heart of service over all the skills in the world. If you stay at the feet of Jesus, servanthood and humility will be alive in your leadership.

GENERATIONAL LEADERSHIP

Jesus lived and led to empower those who were coming behind him. Even Jesus knew that although He was the King and did the work of salvation, He would need the next generation to carry the message. Jesus was patient with them. He was understanding as they learned. Remember, when you're leading, it's not about you—it's always about who is coming behind you. Someone will follow you, and you can influence "next" by taking it seriously now. God's heart is for generations. The trick is to allow God's heart for succeeding generations to become ours. There will always be a next. The next leader, the next pastor, or the next CEO. "Next" is built now. We can't let them down; there is too much at stake. Remember that we are running a marathon, but it's a relay, not a solo race. The heart we steward today will determine the blessings we pass into tomorrow.

Jesus cared so much about all of humanity that would come behind Him. That is why He went to the cross. Jesus knew our hearts needed redemption and did what had to be done. He was obedient to the Father unto the cross. He was selfless, missional, and concerned about the hearts of all humanity. When our hearts care about the ones coming behind us, we make decisions based on truth and wisdom rather than selfishness and pride. Love those who are coming behind you enough to stay at the feet of Jesus, die to self, and sacrifice for who is coming. One of the most significant placements a leader can have is connecting to someone ahead of them and offering a connection to one running behind them. In doing this, you model generational leadership.

SUCCESS VS. SIGNIFICANCE
What is the difference?

> *Success points to your fame, and significance points to His.*

By world standards, there is none. Jesus showed us how to be significant to His Father even when it meant He wasn't successful by the world's standards. The Pharisees and Sadducees thought they had reached the pinnacle of success, and by the world's standards at that time, they had. But to Jesus and His Father's Kingdom, they had failed. If we are going to live like Jesus, we need to make a life of significance our highest aim. Success points to your fame, and significance points to His.

No one understands this better than my friend Jessica. The day Justin and I pulled into town to launch The Avenue, Jessica and her husband Adam were our first phone call. Justin and Adam grew up together; they were more like brothers than friends. When we arrived in Tennessee, it only took one interaction for us to realize that Jessica would be the same—exceptional. I asked her to write the story of her pursuit of success that became one of significance:

> It was a random day of the week, just like any other. The hustle of early morning alarm clocks buzzed, birds chirped outside the window, and hairspray was thick! I found myself face to face with a reflection of the girl I had become. A working mom with a young son, happily married—grinding through life in such a way that was genuinely being shaped by the world.
>
> Until this day.
>
> This day, I was not only met with my reflection but also with an overwhelming feeling of knowing that today, a choice must be made. The overwhelming wisdom that was downloaded in my spirit left me knowing that today, "You will leave all you know in your workplace. The things you went to school for and earned a college degree with . . . you will say goodbye to years of training and investment." This day was a line-in-the-sand moment. I had a choice to make—either choose to stay in what the world called success or step boldly into unknown territory.
>
> At this point, personal success was defined in my mind as owning a home, being married, earning a college degree, having a child, and receiving continual promotions and opportunities in my career. As I am sure you already know, I was wrong! Although I was actively checking the box off in my success column, I was unfulfilled. When you are discontented, you live for the next. We were eager to plan our next vacation, seeking our next pay increase, and buying our next large ticket item. If you have ever found yourself in

this season, it is both exhausting and heavy. There is never enough, and the desire to do more weighs heavy each day.

When God takes hold of your heart and shifts the posture, everything changes. The wisdom that showed up that day was the Holy Spirit speaking to my heart because God had a different plan. He defines success, and He is where joy is found.

See, I knew the Lord. A relationship with Him was planted in me at an early age. Attending church and serving was something I witnessed most of my life and was actively doing at this moment. Although I knew Him and was walking this life out, my heart was set on what the world defined.

He was looking for obedience.

He desired for me to be in unity with His plan.

He wanted to see me truly fulfilled.

He knew there was more, but I had to choose.

God was preparing me in these unfulfilled seasons to be where I am today. Only He could take a girl seeking the world's approval and shift her heart to only desire His. There was no reason to leave my job. I didn't have another one lined up. In fact, I was actively training to receive a promotion in another state.

But God.

He has provided in every season. The major pay decrease I took from walking out in obedience—He found a way to provide the difference. Our family never went without a paycheck. The peace, joy, and fulfillment that flows in our home now is a gift. This was only activated by walking out in obedience to what my heart was telling me. Our minds will talk us out of what we know to be true and attempt to rationalize *in those moments. When God is truly in it, and you take that step of obedience—He meets you right where you are!*

Today our family has grown to trust the Lord more than ever. Through that season, He provided everything we needed. In fact, He supplied more than we needed. He opened doors only He could and orchestrated plans that He gets all the credit for. He ignited passion in our home to seek Him more and become even more generous. He didn't waste anything we had walked through, and because of that obedient heart posture, He was able to use it!

In leadership, we cannot take someone to a place we haven't been. If our hearts are not positioned to walk in obedience and lean into wisdom, we risk leading others in the wrong direction. When the heart is not guided by the Holy Spirit, selfish motives take priority and pride begins to step in. Speaking from personal experience, do not ignore that overwhelming feeling from the Holy Spirit that nudges your heart to activate obedience.

It will take your life from success to significance.

Over the last eleven years, I have seen obedience transform Jessica. She is humble in her presentation. The level at which she lives and leads blesses the Kingdom and everyone around her. Jessica's life points to Jesus. Her ambitions are surrendered to His will. She and Adam have been with us since day one of launching The Avenue; they are so much more than friends. They are family. She is now full-time on our pastoral staff team leading and training leaders. Her joy is infectious, and her heart is as beautiful as the smile that lights up every room she enters. She is significant to my life and significant to the Kingdom. I am grateful for her friendship and leadership. (She is also a driving force behind the *Guarded Brand* for that we are all thankful.)

Don't chase success; chase Jesus.

Choose a life of significance and make Jesus famous. Matthew 16:26 puts significance into perspective by saying, "What good will it be for someone to gain the whole world, yet forfeit their soul? Or what can anyone give in exchange for their soul?" Don't chase success; chase Jesus. Lead people to significance by leading them to the feet of Jesus.

The heart of a good leader recognizes that leadership, like life, is a journey. We will grow, transition into new seasons, and experience gain and loss. But we journey on. Christ showed us how to walk with the Father, and He showed us how to transition. Don't fall in love with what you are leading; fall in love with the One for whom you lead. Stay at the feet of Jesus. Fall on your face and ask God to examine your heart daily, surrender your heart to Him, and lead hidden in Christ.

FINISH THE RACE: GUARD YOUR HEART

Remember the story I shared earlier in this chapter about the fall? From that moment until now, I have worn cute sneakers with almost everything. You don't go through an experience like that without the result of a huge life change. And you don't go through a book like this one without the same. You will want to go back and reflect. As the Holy Spirit highlights a chapter or two, reread it. This process is just the beginning of a new journey. Lace those sneakers up because we have a race to run. It's a marathon. You might take wrong turns sometimes—just turn around. You might have so many changes you want to see in your life that it seems impossible—take it one step at a time. You may feel alone, and if you do, find a journey partner.

Keep your eyes focused on the end goal. One day, at the end of our race, we will see Jesus face to face. He will return to collect the hearts He died to redeem. We will give Him all the praise for the journey. There will be no more heart intruders to guard against. We will offer Him the fruits of our consistency and discipline. The increase will be our offering as we bring others who have changed because of our journey. On that day, we will fall on our face in worship; grateful that we remained GUARDED!

"Guard your heart above all else, for it is the source of life." (HCSB)
"Guard your heart above all else, for it determines the course of your life." (NLT)
"Above all else, guard your heart, for everything you do flows from it." (NIV)
—PROVERBS 4:23

PRAYER OF COMMITMENT

Father, I thank you for showing me how to live a life of significance in you, through your Son. I am committed to fall on my face before you in humility so I don't fail those who follow me. Let others see You in my service, love and leadership. And may I never forget success is only derived when my heart, is hidden in You. It's my desire to live a life that is "Guarded." I welcome your Word to change me and the words that have entered my heart through this book to sharpen me. May my life always bring you honor. In Jesus name, AMEN.

GUARDED REVIEW: PULSE REPORT

1) **Heart Central**
   - Your Heart Your Source
   - Heart and Brain Connections
   - Heart for Jesus
   - Heartbeat
2) **My Heart, My Responsibility**
   - Growing in Responsibility
   - Condition of the Heart: Sin and Heart History
   - Thoughts–Feelings–Choices
     » Knowing and Doing
     » Excuses and Explanation
     » Crush Excuses
3) **Echo**
   - Source: Your Heart—Setting the Standard, Baring the Standard, Communicating the Standard
   - Sound: My Life—How you live; you cannot hide what's inside
   - Symphony: The story of your life—created when all sounds merge

4) **Heart Invaders**
   - Invader Alert: Invaders Operate in Darkness, Invaders Case and Wait
     » Belief Steers Behavior/Boundaries
   - Invader of Fear: Defeated by Faith
   - Invader of Busyness: Blocked by Discipline
   - Invader of Unworthiness: Blocked by Identity in Christ
   - Invader of Unforgiveness: Blocked by Forgiveness
   - Invader of Anxiety and Depression: Blocked by the Peace of God
   - Invader of Apathy: Blocked by Passion
   - Invader of Pride: Blocked by Humility

5) **Heart on Fire**
   - Elements of a Controlled Burn
     » Atmosphere
     » Prescription
     » Boundaries
   - Eternal Flame

6) **Guarded to Gain**
   - The Master of Your Heart (Matthew 25:14-29)
   - Understanding Expectations
   - He Knew Them, They Knew Him
   - Everything to Gain and Everything to Lose
     » A Total Loss: Mind/Sight/Faith/Eternity with Christ
     » Abundant Gain: Trust/Increase—(Abandoned to the Master and the Mission) / Eternal Rewards

7) **Heart Rhythm**
   - Consistency is Key
     » Holy Spirit Empowered /Become a Heart Rhythm/Matter of the Heart
   - Discipline is not a Bad Word
     » Holy Spirit Provided/Corrects the Heart/Protects the Heart

- Close Your Rings: Spiritual/Emotional/Physical

8) **Shame-Free Zone**
    - Jesus Defeated Shame
        - » Shame is defeated, Live in Freedom
            - › Posture Your Heart/Receive the Rain/Open the Flood Gate
            - › Live Your Purpose
            - › Dripping Oil

9) **Matters of the Heart**
    - Constructing Walls vs. Creating Space/Boundaries
    - Trading Spaces
        - » Acquaintances
        - » Friends and Family
    - Close Friends and Family
    - Closest Relationships
        - » Marriage/Children
    - Covenant Friendship
        - » Lifetime Friends/Journey Partners

10) **The Heart of a Leader**
    - We Are All Leaders
        - » Inconvenience vs. Incarceration
    - Fall on Your Face
        - » Servanthood
        - » Generational Leadership
    - Success vs. Significance
    - Finish the Race: Guard Your Heart

MG
Melissa Graham

- PODCAST
- GUARDED COMMUNITY
- BLOG
- CONNECT

SCAN ME!

www.ingramcontent.com/pod-product-compliance
Lightning Source LLC
Chambersburg PA
CBHW050858160426
43194CB00011B/2203